FAITH
QUESTIONS

FAITH QUESTIONS

SEARCHING FOR MEANING AND HOPE

Donagh O'Shea OP

DOMINICAN PUBLICATIONS

First published (2012) by
Dominican Publications
42 Parnell Square
Dublin 1

ISBN 978-1-905604-22-7

British Library Cataloguing in Publications Data.
A catalogue record for this book is available
from the British Library.

Origination by Dominican Publications
Cover design: Bill Bolger
Cover photograph: Donagh O'Shea

Printed in Ireland by
Naas Printing Ltd
South Main Street
Naas, Co. Kildare.

Contents

Introduction

The holiest place on earth, the innermost part of the Temple that Jesus knew, the Holy of Holies ... *exploded*. That explosion was the spiritual equivalent of the Big Bang.

That holiest of all places measured thirty feet in all dimensions. It was totally dark and empty. It was separated from the outside by a veil. Only the high priest was allowed to enter there, once a year. It was the place of meeting with God.

Then it exploded. "Jesus gave a loud cry and breathed his last. And the veil of the temple was torn in two, from top to bottom" (Mark 15:38). In the moments after the explosion the place to see God was in the dying body of Jesus on the cross. He had poured out his life, given everything away, his self-emptying was complete. He was now the Holy of Holies.

As time passed, a new awareness began to dawn in the world, first in the mind of Paul, then spreading among the others. Christ is not alone, he saw. *We are his body.* Through him *we* are now the Holy of Holies. "You are God's temple," he wrote (1 Cor 3:16). Because we have seen God in the broken body of Jesus we can now see God in our own devastated lives. Christ the Light of the world is fractured in ten thousand places, "lovely in eyes not his", lovely in the saints and the half-saints; lovely in the broken lives of the poor and defeated; lovely in the lives of the many who feel lost and abandoned even by the Church.

The conversations in this book reveal some of the anger, the sadness, the disaffection of ordinary people in today's Church, as well as their enduring search for hope and meaning. Live conversations are much more than an exchange of ideas; they are the full presence of people to one another, ideally with warmth in their voices and kindness in their eyes. On the printed page these qualities are hidden, but at least there are still presences, however shadowed. People have put questions to me, sometimes face to face, sometimes by mail or email, and waited for a response. In some cases the questions grew into extended conversations. I was persuaded by a few friends to put some of these conversations into print. Most of the material is taken from my website www.goodnews.ie

Conversation has seldom been so necessary for us, because in every way the world is becoming increasingly polarised, and with it the Church. There is disintegration at many levels as people drift further apart. In the Church there are some who think they are doing God a service by deepening these divides. But while we still talk to one another there is hope. The *Logos* is the assurance that our chaos is a universe still. Despite the shades of darkness, the light that is Christ is still shining and expanding in the lives of millions of people.

God

To believe or disbelieve

I find it harder and harder to believe in God. I don't mean that I've been thinking about proofs of his existence and saying, "No, that one doesn't work, and neither does that," and concluding that there is no God. It's more that the whole idea looks ready to fall away by itself, like Santa Claus. Even without existing, come to think of it, God could still do a lot of good, like Santa Claus! And I suspect that a lot of people who say they believe in God, don't really. But you must do, since you're putting up this stuff on the net and getting nothing for it. Do you believe rock-solid in the existence of God, and do you never even for a minute suspect that maybe … just maybe … there's nothing up there?

If there were some facts that might prove the existence of God, or some other facts that might disprove it, we could try to sort out the two kinds. But for someone who believes in God everything proves (or rather shows, or is consistent with) the existence of God, while for someone who doesn't, everything equally fails to do so. The claim is that God is the creator of *all* that exists, so *in the nature of the case* nothing could count against God's existence. But equally, that is just what removes the basis of all argument, for and against. Your question takes me out of my depth, as it takes every believer. We have *knowledge* of many things, but very little *proof* in a strict sense. These two are quite different, and people sometimes discover this distinction for the first time in a courtroom. But when you look closely you can discover it almost every moment. It is a theme that will keep recurring.

There are probably very few people who stop believing in God because of a purely intellectual argument. It is much more common for belief in God just to slip, like a coat slipping off the shoulder; or like belief in Santa Claus, as you say. In fact, the loss of belief in Santa Claus could be a practice run for the other! I remember a famous description by Sartre of his own loss of belief. I have it here. "One morning in 1917, at La Rochelle, I was waiting for some companions who were supposed to accompany me to the lycée; they were late. Soon I could think of nothing more to distract myself, and I decided to think about the Almighty. He at once tumbled down into the blue sky and vanished without explanation…. I have never since had the least inclination to revive him." It was the same Sartre who was to write the influential book *Being and Nothingness*.

I'm sorry for quoting passages from writers, but I want you to see that I'm not just concocting ideas to meet your question. May I bring up the words of a writer who was more than a writer – a man who was ablaze with God, if ever there was one. Meister Eckhart said in the fourteenth century:

> Anything you see, or anything that comes within your ken, that is not God, because God is neither this nor that. Whoever says God is here or there, do not believe him. The light that God is, shines in the darkness. God is the true light: to see it, one must be blind and must strip from God all that is 'something'. A master says: whoever speaks of God in any likeness, speaks impurely of Him. But to speak of God with nothing is to speak of Him correctly. When the soul is unified and there enters into total self-abnegation, then she finds God as in Nothing. It appeared to a man as in a dream – it was a waking dream – that he became pregnant with Nothing like a woman with child, and in that Nothing God was born, God was the fruit of Nothing. God was born in the Nothing.

This is the only passage in which Eckhart referred to his own enlightenment, or in fact to himself at all. It is startling language, but it is normal with the Christian mystics, as with mystics of every religion. The famous seven-times repeated *"nada"* of St John of the Cross is the best-known example, but there are countless others. Nothing. God has to fall away!

God as object has to tumble down into the blue sky. Many people smile at the idea of the Old Man in the Sky with the White Beard. But any idea of God as object comes to the same thing. While we continue to imagine God as a kind of object – a super-object, of course! – the language of objects will do. Millions of people have become so dissatisfied with 'God as object' that they almost know what an atheist feels, and they think that they are therefore atheists. God as an object: *obiectum,* 'something thrown against'. That kind of God would be a limited God, an idol. But when you deny God as object someone will say you are making God 'subjective'. But it is not a case of denying one side of a distinction in favour of the other. It is a case, rather, of denying the distinction itself. God leaps over that distinction.

So, to answer your question, do I suspect that there may be nothing up there? There are lots of objects up there, but I'm not tempted to think of God as one of them. Every day of my life I'm drawn to prayer and meditation: I go willingly; I get up early in the morning to do it. Everything I do during the day seems shallow if I miss it. What do I do while I'm sitting there for a couple of hours every day? Nothing! And when I catch myself doing something I stop it! Something in me is trying to come more awake. I intend to stay there every morning and evening for the rest of my life. That's my search for God ... such as it is. It couldn't possibly be the only way, but it's mine, and it's the way of many people. I could pass the time looking at myself, the subject; or I could pass the time thinking about the Object. But I will try to stay in that clear 'space' where the ego has nothing to project and nothing to project onto. I believe that that space is the Christ-nature in us. He is still struggling to be born.

Jargon

Why is the Christian religion so hard to understand? For no particular reason I looked up predestination on the net – or it may be I looked it up because it was the hardest word I remember in religion. Whenever I try to get deeper into religion I'm hit with a volley of impossible words. When I looked up predestination I got these beauties (I wrote them down). Omniscience, determ inism, supralapsarianism (wow!), infralapsarianism, immanence, transcen- dence, premotion.... How many people know what those words mean? Can I get deeper into my religion without studying all that stuff...? I thought Christianity was for everyone.

Yes, it is for everyone – including people who addle their brains with supralapsarianism, etc. But these would be quite a small constituency. The Christian faith is very ancient; it has spread and developed in many different cultures since the beginning. Instead of trying to be a self-contained package, it has always tried to integrate with each culture in which it found itself: theologically, philosophically, socially, every way (with varying degrees of success). And so, much of the language of theology reflects debates that were vital in their time, but are now long-forgotten (by everyone except professors of theology). Every one of those issues is fascinating, if you had time to go into it. Many of them may not be worth the time and effort.

Not everyone who tries to unravel predestination will enter the king-dom of heaven. There's no mention of it in the gospels. It was a theological question that occurred to people centuries later, as they reflected on the Gospel. I'm aware that your question isn't about predestination as such, but about whether depth necessarily leads to complexity.

I don't think it does. The deepest things are utterly simple. That's what makes them difficult to grasp. Up to a point, we are more at home with complexity than we are with simplicity. A complex notion (like a complex object) can be taken apart and examined piece by piece, but a simple notion has no parts: it has to be grasped whole. For example, if we weren't so used to zero in arithmetic, we would find it very difficult to grasp. You can imagine ancient people asking, "Why do we need a symbol for *nothing*?" In religion too they talk about 'Nothing', but I'll come to that.

It struck me forcibly once when I was celebrating the Eucharist with a group of people, that we would not be here doing this thing if Jesus had not walked the roads of Palestine. Each of us would be somewhere else, doing something else; we would not be praying these prayers or saying these things to one another, nor sitting, standing, moving in the way we do; this building would not be here, arranged in the way it is.... Nothing but the *fact* of Jesus makes sense of what we are doing. This makes him as present and as real as the walls around us and the roof overhead. The roads he walked lead to here. There is no separation, no distance. His sandals are lined up with ours. There is no abstraction; it is all as *concrete* as anything could be.

It doesn't matter now whether we are infra- or supralapsarians. What matters – and what has always mattered – is the presence of Jesus in us and between us, and in everything we do. This presence isn't something you can check out with instruments; it is spiritual presence – which means *real* presence, not something imagined. If someone knew the whole history of the debates about predestination but didn't know this presence, he or she would not have entered into any depth of the Christian faith.

Sometimes a Christian has moments when the mind is clear of all thinking and there is just presence. It is an awareness so free of the clutter of thinking that the mystics have spoken of it as an experience of 'Nothing'. It's not that there is nothing there! It is that there is no thinking there; there is nothing to say because there is no distance. Meister Eckhart spoke about becoming "pregnant with Nothing". To get passing glimpses of what he experienced is much more important than to become entangled in the thoughts of people who may never have had that experience at all.

What I would suggest is that you develop an eye for the things that are so simple and so constant that we usually don't notice them at all. This is the path that leads into the depth of our religion.

God and emptiness

I cannot feel God's love. And if God is love then perhaps I cannot find God.... Christianity beckoned to me because it acknowledged and accepted me as I was and even embraced my failure. But as I have studied the great mystics like Eckhart I have begun to see that what they were talking about is awfully like the Buddhism I left behind. It was precisely the instruction to abandon the self completely that so confounded me as a Buddhist.... Where was the God who accepted me for who I am now, warts and all...?

I am beginning to wonder if I have been deceiving myself. Christianity is not an easier, more comforting route. The work that needs to be done is the same in any language and God's love is perhaps not like any kind of love I am familiar with. But once more I am left with my own failure. I don't run from it so much these days but I can't seem to get beyond it. Life seems bleak and hopeless and God has become something remote, unreachable, even hostile.... Where is God's love in all this?

"Act as if everything depended on you," said St Augustine, "knowing that everything depends on God." If you were to try to live by just one part of that sentence – whether the first part or the second – you would be on a very uncertain road. If you were simply to say, "Everything depends on God," you would not be inclined to make any effort at all. You would then be unable (or unwilling) to internalise and make my own what God has given freely and for nothing. On the other side, if you were to say, "Everything depends on me," you would feel crushed with responsibility and feelings of failure. This second position seems to be where you are at present.

So, St Augustine's 'map' suggests that you might take the direction of 'Everything depends on God'. In every genuine spirituality this comes into focus sooner or later – even when people don't use the language of Christians. Nobody can enlighten him or herself. Any enlightenment that comes your way comes as a complete surprise, not as the completion of a project – even when you have been working hard towards it. Some famous teacher once said, "I was never enlightened!" This came as a surprise to many of his students – until he spelled it out. The 'I' – the ego – never becomes enlightened. Enlightenment is precisely joyful freedom from this 'I', freedom from the ego's control. Enlightenment is what is there when the ego isn't; it is one's true nature, which lies deeper than the ego.

In Christian terms this is "dying to oneself" (see John 12:24-25). Because we remember the way Jesus died we tend to think of this as an awful experience. But it means being freed of a false narrow identity and being drawn into a deeper life in Christ – an experience of great joy. 'Emptiness', 'nothingness', 'the void' … these terrifying words are not what they seem. They are not suggesting that there is really nothing out there. They are not statements about external reality at all. They are about the mind that is free of ego: free of the urge to be selfishly independent, to be in fact one's own god.

The gospels leave us in no doubt, Christianity is for sinners. The parable of the Prodigal Son (Luke 15) is deeply moving, unforgettable. Jesus could have put together any kind of story he wanted; he could have put in lots of qualifications; he could have concluded, as religious story-tellers mostly do, with a great deal of moralising. But he did none of this. The parable stands there on the page, totally free. It was Jesus' way of describing the mercy of God. It is this that encourages us to keep on trying, even when we have failed over and over. God embraces us just as we are, and doesn't wait till we improve. This is a source of great joy and encouragement.

Christians use the language of human relationships when speaking about God. Father and Son. Not Prime Mover, not Emanation, not Life Force, not Energy…. This should prevent our spirituality from becoming cold and impersonal. (Of course it doesn't always do so, when people's human relationships are troubled; but it is meant to do so.) Even when Christian mystics speak about "the dark night of the soul," or about God as "Nothing" (St John of the Cross and Meister Eckhart), the language of human relationships is not put aside but deepened and widened. They are saying that God is our Father in a way that surpasses any thought or image or experience that we have ever had. You wrote, "God's love is perhaps not like any kind of love I am familiar with." Yes, because God is not a creature. But human love is a distant *pointer* to God's love. When the Christian mystics use negative language, saying God is *not* this and *not* that, what they are denying of God is not the quality itself (love, for example) but the human limitation in it. "God is love," St John wrote – and we know it has to be love beyond our imagining.

"Life seems bleak and hopeless," you wrote, "and God has become something remote, unreachable, even hostile." I really hope and pray, David, that this painful part of your journey will soon lead onto a wide open joyful path, where you will know that when God moves beyond your reach, it is to lead you on, not to abandon you. As a practical thing to do, I would suggest that you read that story of the Prodigal Son every day. In fact the whole of chapter 15 of Luke's gospel is parables about being lost and found: the lost sheep, the lost coin, the lost son. If you read it often enough your reading will move beyond reading and become a kind of immersion.

God: far or near?

I have a question that has been going around in my head for a long time now. You often quote Meister Eckhart and other mystics. I'm reading St John of the Cross, and I begin to wonder how their emphasis on the unknowability of God and on Nothing and Emptiness can be squared with the Word made flesh and living among us. When St. Paul tried to preach about the Unknown God people laughed at him. And he made a decision there and then to preach no more that way, but only to preach about "Jesus Christ and him crucified." As they said to St Paul on that occasion, "we would like to hear you talk about this again." Any comments would be appreciated.

Your question touches the central nerve of Christian spirituality. I'll mark out a few lines as best I can, and hope that something there will suggest a way forward for your own reflection.

It can seem like two different religions: one of them cold and esoteric, the other warm and human. It might seem that they could get on quite well without each other, but I'll try to say why that isn't so.

The mystery of Jesus is that he is mediator; this means that he "spans the vast abyss" between God and humanity. St Catherine of Siena called him the bridge. A bridge has to remain fixed to both sides. There would be no special mystery to Jesus if he wasn't also divine. In leaving the Father's side he did not cease to be divine. So we can never dismiss consideration of the transcendence of God. The Incarnation does not diminish it in any way; it makes it *accessible* – which is different. St Paul used this word. "Christ Jesus our Lord in whom we have *access* to God" (Ephesians 3:12).

The paradoxes that follow from this are everywhere. The poems of John of the Cross are as sensuous in their imagery and feeling as the *Song of Songs* on which they are styled. Yet it was by way of a line-by-line commentary on these poems that he wrote about "the dark night of the soul," and about *Nada* – 'Nothing'. On the fly-leaf of his *Ascent of Mount Carmel* he drew a sketch of the spiritual journey, and along the central path he wrote *'Nada'* seven times. Before the seventh he wrote, "Even on the summit of Mount Carmel" (by which he meant the peak of spiritual development) – *"Nada."* This paradox lived in the small physical frame of St John of the Cross, and he never weakened one side to strengthen the other.

Meister Eckhart likewise gave strong expressions of this paradox. "God is in all things, the more God is in things the more God is out of things ... the more in the more out and the more out the more in." This may sound a little obscure until we realise he is speaking about transcendence and immanence. The more transcendent God is, the more immanent; and the more immanent the more transcendent. Transcendence is about the unknowability of God; it says God is other than all creatures and beyond our capacity to grasp. Immanence is about the presence of God in everything. These, as I said, may seem to be two different religions, but Eckhart is saying that they necessarily work together: "the more in the more out...." Not the more in the less out.

An image came to me that could clarify this. Imagine a hospital ward with ten beds in a row and one very active and attentive nurse who is present to every one of the ten patients. She is able to be present to them all *because she is not one of them*. In a sense, she is 'transcendent' to them. But imagine then that one day she herself becomes ill and is placed in an eleventh bed in the same ward. She may appear to be nearer to the patients now, since she is one of them; but in fact she is not, she is farther away from them because now she can be present only to herself. In some such way God is intimate to every creature *because* God is transcendent to all creatures.

These are general considerations. When it comes to Jesus, what is added? Beyond the intimacy that creatures have with the transcendent God, Jesus is "one in being with the Father". This cannot be said of any other being. But God is not diminished in Jesus; God remains transcendent – transcendent, but accessible, tangible, in Jesus. "What we have heard, what we have seen with our eyes, what we have looked at and touched with our hands...." When we look at Jesus we are looking into the abyss that is God. We still cannot grasp that abyss – how could a creature grasp infinity? – but we have the courage and even a certain right to stand there in knowing presence, because we are one with Christ in his Body.

As I understand it, St Paul on the Areopagus was trying to engage the Athenians in a sort of apologetics, or 'natural theology' as it used to be called. It was not theology at all, but philosophy. It failed then, and it fails now. Philosophy may open you to the idea of God, but it cannot bring you to faith. The few grudging scraps that a philosopher might allow a believer could never be on a par with the seeming 'agnosticism' of the mystics. The first is showing you the limits of 'proof', the second is showing you the limits of knowledge.

God the Father

I live with a feminist and I never stop hearing about sexism.... In the Catholic Church, she says, patriarchalism goes all the way to the top because the church even sees God as a male. To be honest I feel a bit on the defensive at times. To tease her I tell her that God can't help it if he's male, any more than I can, but that annoys her. I'd like to be able to ease her mind a bit if that's possible. Is there anything I can say that would help her instead of annoying her?

There are many passages in the Bible and in Christian tradition that use feminine images of God. Giving God exclusively male attributes is only a habit, and your friend is right to be annoyed by it.

"God created humankind in his image, in the image of God he created them; male and female he created them" (Genesis 1:27, NRSV translation). This means that male and female persons are equally images of God, and are therefore equally entitled to imagine God in terms of their own gender. (We'll come to the pronoun 'he' later.)

To use only male images of God is to restrict the image of God in humanity – to rob God of the distinctive way in which God is imaged in women. Exclusively female images, of course, would equally restrict God's image in humanity. If we were to react by excluding all gender words, we would not eliminate the problem but double it: our images of God would become amorphous and impersonal. God is beyond gender, but we are not. God-talk (a fair translation of the word 'theology') doesn't have to decide whether we should use male or female images of God – any more than we have to decide whether the human race is male or female. The challenge is to use both – just as the human challenge is to enable men and women to complement each other.

Make a list of so-called masculine images: strength, ruler, leader, provider, power…. And a list of so-called feminine images: grace, tenderness, care, affection, beauty…. I say 'so-called' because these are not the exclusive property of either gender – even if some of them are unevenly distributed. The challenge for all of us is to integrate the qualities that we expect to find in the opposite sex. Who would want to exclude any of these qualities from our language about God?

Make a search through the Scriptures for feminine traits in God; among them you will find the following from Isaiah: "Can a woman forget her nursing-child, or show no compassion for the child of her womb? Even these may forget, yet I will not forget you" (49:15). "As a mother comforts her child, so I will comfort you; you shall be comforted in Jerusalem" (66:13). But what about the 'he' you find in the Old Testament? There are no gender-neutral pronouns in Hebrew; everything is a 'he' or a 'she'. For example, *hayyah* (the word for an animal) is a feminine noun, but this does not mean that the animal in question is always female. *Sefer* (a book) is always masculine…. and so on. All this is true of many languages. The words for God (*Elohim, Adonai*) are masculine nouns in Hebrew, so God is called 'he'. On the other hand the 'Spirit of God' (*Ruach Elohim*) is feminine, and so is *Shekhinah* – 'Presence of God'. In Greek, the word for God (*theos*) is masculine, and the word for Spirit (*pneuma*) is neuter. In brief, the gender of words has nothing to do with the gender of what the words refer to.

In many languages the masculine becomes the default pronoun. But in Tagalog, I'm told, there is only one word for 'he' and 'she': *siya* (pronounced 'she – a'). No doubt this is why Filipinos who speak perfect English will still occasionally make the mistake of referring to a man as 'she'. English does not have such a word, so we just have to do our best not to limit our awareness of God to one half of its range.

Your friend might look at the classics of Christian spirituality. Meister Eckhart repeatedly uses phrases like: "God takes the greatest delight in giving birth." "The Father's name is 'giving birth'." "God is forever on the birth-couch giving birth." And of course Julian of Norwich's book: "God rejoices to be our Father, and God rejoices to be our Mother, and God rejoices to be our true spouse, and that our soul is his beloved wife." Notice that while including both masculine and feminine she doesn't bother herself about the pronoun 'he'. It's only a word, and for her (unlike many who insist on it now) it doesn't carry any sexist baggage. I can send your friend some extended passages if she is interested. At any rate, it will be good for her to know that they exist.

Sexism in the Church is a whole other story, and someone is bound to ask me that question; but your question was about God.

Searching for God

I've been searching for God for eight years, I mean really searching. I wouldn't be what you would call a practising Catholic, but I read a lot. I read book after book, but I don't seem to be getting anywhere. I even began to read Meister Eckhart, but he left me completely at sea. I could hardly get through the first page. Then someone told me I was reading the wrong Eckhart, I should be reading Eckhart Tolle. The Power of Now *is a great book, but he hardly ever mentions God.... Could you recommend some other book that would help me here? I don't intend to give up, but I'm finding the going very rough.*

All searching for God is already a kind of finding. "All the way to God is God," said St Teresa of Ávila. Don't be impatient to come to the end of your search. That might conceal a hidden wish to be simply rid of it. The search for God doesn't end. If you were to see, for example, an 80-year-old monk in his monastery you might get the impression that he had long ago come to the end of his search. But the ancient monastic prescription is "to seek God" – *quaerere Deum* – all one's life. We seek God all our life long. So settle down for the long haul!

I could not do better here than quote Rilke for you, though in this passage he was not referring specifically to the search for God.

> Have patience with everything unresolved in your heart and try to love the questions themselves, as if they were rooms or books written in a very foreign language. Don't search for the answers, which could not be given to you now, because you would not be able to live them. And the point is to live everything. Live the question now. Perhaps then, some day far in the future you will gradually, without even noticing it, live your way into the answer.

I think Rilke would like to wean you away a little from books, and so would I. Books are wonderful, like food; they are a kind of food. Eating and reading are good in moderation – when we take a bit of exercise afterwards! Spiritual practice is walking with God. The book I would recommend is the book of experience.

How do we walk with God? By seeing God in everything, because "God is in all things". Does that mean that when you look at something you don't see it at all, but instead you start thinking about God? No, no, that would be to say that God is not in things at all, that God is only an external reference. We don't have to *think* about God in order to be present to God. This is not to say that thinking about God is useless. No, it has many uses; but God is present to us in ways that are "too deep for words" (Romans 8:26), too deep for thinking. God is in all things, we say. God has no problem being present; *we* are the ones who have trouble being present. When we are present in this moment of our own life we are present to God. To walk in our true reality is to walk with God.

Here is a way in. Sit beside a tree. Resist the temptation to start quoting lines of poetry about it, or even to think about it. Just look. Look at it in the way a baby looks at things (you may have to look at a baby first, to see how this is done!). See the majesty of the tree, its shape, its great strength, its constancy and stability, its innocence and truthfulness, its defencelessness; hear its silence. Stay with it and let nothing separate you from it; *be one with it*. Now think: what was it in you that made those qualities in the tree perceptible to you? Clearly, the same qualities in yourself. (A man with a chainsaw would see the tree differently.) *What you see is the way you see it*. If you have any experience that God is in you, you will see God in everything.

Eckhart Tolle's books and talks are compelling because they keep recalling us to presence. Just now, as I was typing, the Angelus bell rang and I did what I always do: I stood in silence for the duration and let the sound of the bell go right through me, cleaning me out and leaving a silence in which the mystery of the Incarnation can echo. Eckhart Tolle doesn't mention God much, as you say. This, he said, is because the word 'God' has become so used and so misused that for many it can now stand as a barrier to awareness rather than as an expression of it. Christian mystics have said the same thing – the other Eckhart, for example, once said: "I pray God to rid me of God!" Words can become idols, as believers have always known – even the word 'God'. They are much more likely to be mistaken for the reality than a statue or a picture. "If one knows anything in God," said Meister Eckhart, "and affixes any name to it, that is not God. God is above names."

To sum up, then: how then do we see God in all things? We search for God all our lives; but God is not lost. *We* are lost. God is always present, and when we become present God is present in that awareness. As long as we are present – to anything, even to a tree – we are present to God. Any object, any sound, anything whatsoever, can clean us out, as the Angelus bell does, and leave a silence in which the Silent Presence can reverberate.

Trying to believe

I am a non-believer trying to believe. Like the two on the road to Emmaus, my heart burns when I hear Christians speak of their experiences; but I'm afraid that what I'm really feeling is envy/self-pity because I cannot feel I will ever belong. My problem is that whenever I feel – or imagine I feel – the presence of God (usually when I try praying/meditating) the question that keeps nagging at me is: Am I trying to believe in God because I need to ? and not because I know he exists? My greatest fear is that I will never move beyond this doubt. I was encouraged by the title to one of your retreats recently, 'The Obstacles are the Path'. Is there is a way around this obstacle for me?

When you say you are "a 'non-believer' desperately trying to believe", I'm reminded of the man in the gospel who said, "I believe; help my unbelief!" (Mark 9:24). In both cases belief and unbelief are mixed together, though differently. Still, from your letter it seems clear enough that you are already a believer, struggling to deepen your faith. That is a noble struggle, and not something to be ashamed of.

Don't be anxious: no one, if they are honest, can be 100% sure of their motives. I have the deepest distrust of people who scream conviction at us; I always have the feeling that it is fuelled by its exact opposite. Such people are shouting to convince *themselves*, because they are afraid to look at their own uncertainties. The world is filling up with such fundamentalists. Faith is not a conviction that we dredge up from our own resources, but a gift from God. To the extent that it really is a gift, it is received with humility and gratitude, and spoken of with respect and wonder. That may sound like a number of platitudes, but it is what lifts faith above the commotion of our own moods and feelings, and gives it a serene unconditional quality. Even in the absence of any special experiences or feelings I may have very strong faith – much stronger, it may be, than the faith of someone who relies on experiences or feelings. I would suggest, Patricia, that you pay no heed at all at present to other people's accounts of their experiences. Even if these experiences are authentic, they are personal to those people and have nothing to do with you. Read the gospels yourself and let your heart be touched by the great heart of Christ. Continue to pray and meditate in your own way, and be faithful to what arises there for you.

You say you take two steps forwards and one step backwards. That means that at least you are moving, you are not clinging like a fundamentalist. Faith means trust. A fundamentalist doesn't trust at all; he clings, and he hates everything that moves. The great irony is that people who cling are inclined to think that they have really firm faith. But you are moving, trusting, trying to trust. Can we be sure which way is backwards and which is forwards? Success and failure have their ordinary definitions reversed by the Cross of Christ. What I call success may well be a failure, and *vice versa*.

You said, "I cannot feel I will ever belong." The need to belong, though it is basic in human nature, frequently leads people astray. It is quite ambiguous in itself. Many of the greatest Christians have experienced profound rejection, even by their own. But before their minds, no doubt, stood the image of Christ on the Cross, rejected and betrayed, yet mysteriously raised up by the Father. His death and resurrection were the origin of the New Community, the Church. That Community was born out of extreme isolation; it was not the fruit of group psychology, but of the Spirit. Real belonging is never simple. Gradually you will recognise the community of faith, but don't make a feeling of belonging a precondition.

Likewise, don't worry about feeling the presence of God. Feelings, like the need to belong, are quite ambiguous. Without them, it's true, we would be like robots, but they have no compass of their own: they can lead us in any and every direction. Just be faithful to what is given you in prayer and meditation, and it will grow.

"Am I trying to believe in God because I need to, and not because I know he exists?" Yes, that is a constant question for believers: what are my motives, as far as I can discern them, for believing in God? If I were to think that my belief in God was just a thing organised by my own mind, then I would have every reason to be doubtful about it. But it is more than that. Compare if, if you like, to the instinct a salmon has to return to the place of its origin. That 'knowledge' of its origins is not something that the salmon worked out for itself; it is more like the opposite: it is knowledge that is working (almost by itself) in the salmon. The salmon certainly "needs" to get back to its origin, but this need doesn't make it a false effort. In my search for God I may indeed be driven forward by my neediness, my emptiness…. But that doesn't make it a false search. Without that spur I may not bother to seek God at all. For another person, it may be a sense of exuberance that brings them to God. It hardly matters. Keep to your own path, and "go with God."

– 2 –

The Church

Time to give up on it?

Can you answer me a simple question: Why should anyone bother with the Church any more? There's only so much we can take. I haven't given up but I'm considering it. A fair number of my friends don't go to Mass anymore. Why bore ourselves to death – is there some benefit in boredom? People can do a lot of good without ever going to Mass, and some people who do go have done a lot of harm. In fairness I know there are lots of good people too in the Church, but they would be good wherever they were. Will the churches be empty in a few years?

Let me tell you of an experience I had a few months ago. College chaplains in Ireland invited me to take part in their annual conference, even though I'm not a college chaplain. Instead of inviting someone to give them lectures they decided they would go as a group to various places in Dublin where people were actually living the Gospel rather than just talking about it.

First on the list was Peter McVerry, S.J., who has been taking care of homeless people in Dublin for more than 30 years, advocating tirelessly for them and organising help. He never raises the question of religion with them; he has to *embody* faith hope and love, he said, rather than talk about them. One young man, a recovering drug addict, pointed to Peter and said, "If it wasn't for this man I would certainly be dead." We went from there to 'Kevin's Kitchen': Kevin is a Capuchin brother who has been running a day care centre since 1969, where he manages to give a full Irish breakfast to around 250 disadvantaged people every morning, and between 400 and 500 full dinners every day. Every week his centre hands out about 1,000 bags of groceries to the poor. He is helped by an army of volunteers, and countless people who give financial support. I saw teenagers washing enormous piles of plates, who might find it hard to wash a mug at home. When something genuine is being done, people join in willingly. Brother Kevin says he always gives his clients the very best he can get. For their whole lives these people had been feeling that they were second-best. Giving them something second-best would just confirm that feeling. Next day we went to Sr Stanislaus Kennedy's centre. Like Peter McVerry, she has been organising and working for decades to combat the effects of poverty and homelessness. From there we went to 'Sophia Housing'. Many years ago the Sisters of Mercy donated a convent to a group who developed it into housing for homeless women. What strikes you instantly is the beauty of the place. This, the Sister said, is a way of telling those women that they are not second-best. By the way, all these places I have mentioned have websites where you can get information on what they do.

These are the peaks, but there are vast foothills: countless people who have a heart and who look after one another: carers, helpers, volunteers, good fathers and mothers, decent struggling people, the overwhelming majority. The work has been going on unseen, unofficial and unannounced. "My Father goes on working, and so do I" (John 5:17). Most of the work of the Church happens below the radar.

I found those three days deeply moving, and I came home convinced that you have to look in the right places to find the Church. You find it where the Gospel is being lived. All that work of service to the disadvantaged is done below the radar: right on the ground, on the street, in the home. All the struggles of ordinary Catholics are carried on below the radar.

Above the radar what do you get? The big hats and the big egos. It is a big mistake to identify the Church with the hierarchy. The Church is Christ together with all the members of his body – all of us. That's why it is worth staying with it. Don't let anyone's behaviour deprive you of your identity. That would be to give them absolute power over you.

The Church is going through a trial by fire at the present time. That fire will burn away everything that is not genuine – clericalism and pomp and wealth and control – but the genuine things will last. A crisis of these dimensions can help bring us back to a real sense of who the Church is, and what can withstand scrutiny and what cannot. Even in the worst situations something good is coming into focus. That would be in keeping with the logic of the faith: from death comes resurrection and new life.

Organised religion

I suppose I'm a bit alienated from all institutions – and more than a bit! Organisations, parties, movements – they all leave me cold. When I see anything like that I want to run the other way. But the Church is the oldest organisation of all. I don't know how there's anyone still in it. At the same time I believe in the spiritual side of life – it means a lot to me in a way I can't spell out very well. It's the deepest part of a person. But why does that have to be tied up then in an institution? What have institutions got to do with it? They're only interested in their pecking order and in promoting themselves. I can't see Jesus in any of that. What do you say?

Years ago, Alan Watts wrote (I'm quoting from memory, but quite accurately I believe) that the Church has in her possession, as in a trunk, the purest mystical wisdom, but she isn't opening it up for the world – because of the sheer weight of so many clerical gentlemen sitting on the lid. Most, I would add, don't know that they are sitting on anything; they are just not evoking a level of experience that they ought to be evoking, not mediating the mystery: not mediating it even to themselves. Nothing is so much out of a man's sight as what he is sitting on. You have every right to complain and to walk away wherever you see that.

What do I say? The institution and the spirit are always in tension. But there's good and bad tension.

There's the kind of tension that diminishes people, that frays their nerves and wears them down, that dulls their idealism and prevents miracles. Even Jesus couldn't work in that atmosphere. "He *could not* do any miracles there," Mark said (6:5). (It was his home village, and the people wanted to keep him in his place: a village is often the worst kind of institution.) Yes, we all know many institutions that are interested only in controlling people. The control-freak rises to the top, setting up and reinforcing patterns of dependency that reduce rather than enlarge people.

But there's another kind of tension: the kind that is part of all life. The word 'organisation' suggests bureaucracy and machine-like efficiency. But of course it comes from the word 'organic'. It is a metaphor from nature, and not from the mechanical world. Nature is seldom chaotic; it is highly structured at every level. The spirit too needs structure. It even needs difficulties and constraints, and it dissipates itself if it doesn't find any. Imagine a wide lazy river with no banks: it just spreads out wherever it wants; it is going nowhere in particular, it has no depth or power; it just evaporates in the sun. Imagine the depth and the power it would have if it were flowing between banks (the narrower the banks, in fact, the more depth and power). This is how I interpret Jesus's saying that the gate to life is narrow. "Enter through the narrow gate; for wide is the gate and broad is the road that leads to destruction, and many enter through it" (Matthew 7:13).

"The Church, like any organisation, has to have rules; and if people don't want to keep the rules they should get out!" I have heard that depressing judgment more than once, and seen it often in print. I wonder if the person who says such a thing would say the same about his own bodily organs – his kidneys, for example, or his liver, or his heart – when they become troublesome.

Every Church community is part of the Body of Christ, but sometimes it operates more like a power-structure that robs and diminishes you instead of enriching and enlarging you. What a tragedy it is, and how far from the original intention! Writing in the fifth century about the Eucharist, St Augustine said, "All of that is about you! The mystery being celebrated on the altar is the mystery of you. You became Christ's body and his members [at baptism], when you said, 'Amen!' to that mystery of what you are. Now also in the Eucharist you receive his Body and you say, 'Amen!'"

To look back even closer to the origin: an ancient book called the *Didachè,* written in the first century was discovered in 1883. It contains an account of the Eucharist and the words that were used then. Here is one sentence of it. "As this broken bread, once dispersed over the hills, was brought together and became one loaf, so may your Church be brought together from the ends of the earth into your Kingdom." It is a beautiful image. The grains of wheat were gathered from the fields and hillsides and made into this one loaf; likewise the people, whose homes are scattered all over the hills, have come together to form one community – one Bread, one Body of Christ. And may that gathering be endlessly wider and deeper, till Kingdom come!

Christian community grows out of the Eucharist, not out of canon law, and never out of power politics and mechanical systems of control. It would be hard, I think, to extract 'spirituality' from canon law. But the Eucharist is an endless spiritual resource. Even a simple part of it like the Sign of Peace is full of meaning. On the surface it may be just a winter handshake with a stranger in a badly heated church. But its deepest meaning says: I don't know your name or anything about you, but in the broken body of Christ I would lay down my life for you.

One true Church

May I make a point that may not seem very civil? I hope you can take questions like this, and not be shocked or offended by them. No offence is intended. Sometimes I'm close to giving up when I hear clerical gentlemen claiming that the Catholic Church is the only authentic Church there is and that Christianity is superior to all other religions (described as "gravely deficient"). They claim they are defending Christ and his work, but I wonder if they know how it turns people away? Religion is made to seem a cheap self-advertising thing. If it wasn't for two or three examples of real sanctity I would be gone. I'm blessed in knowing a few genuinely saintly people, and everything about them proves that real religion is exactly the opposite of claim and brazen as-

sertion. It's hard not to sound angry, but I'm not so much angry as troubled
and disillusioned. Despite everything, I am looking for a way of surviving
in the Catholic Church, but I want to live in it without that kind of claim
being made on my behalf.

I know that you are very far from being alone: I have been asked your
question many times. I've been trying to reflect on it for some time, in-
adequately but as well as I can. I offer you the following brief instalment.
But please don't be limited by my limitations.

At heart the language of religion is a language of love, not a language
of objects. Objects are 'out there', distinct from the 'subject' (the thinker
or speaker) – even in the case where we are thinking about ourselves. In
other words this kind of knowledge creates a distinction between subject
and object. But a language of love is a language of union or communion;
love makes us *one* – even while we know perfectly well that the loved
one is a different person (or thing). "If God were in me and I were not
in God, or if I were in God and God were not in me, there would be
two," said Meister Eckhart. God and I are not two, he says; God is not
a reality that can be counted along with a creature. We are not two. But
neither are we one in being. We are one in love.

There has been a lop-sided emphasis on dogma. The deepest cause of
boredom in the Church, I believe, is this endemic rationalism that fails to
nourish the spirit or even the imagination. People are bored because the
Faith is presented to them as a *finished product* (like the modern child's
toy). All we are called to do is to declare it ours. There are more 'theo-
logicians' than theologians: the Word of God, the *logos* is not moving in
them, but only the categories of logic. That bias is not limited to academic
theologians; it is visible everywhere and at every level. A couple of years
ago I read this in the preface to a liturgical calendar: "We are greatly
helped not only by theological investigation but also by that heritage that
is the lived theology of the saints." This one sentence stands out in my
memory as a perfect expression of that same rationalism. Theological
reflection, it seemed to say, is first and last; and the sanctified life is just
an illustration of theology! Reflection is first, and only then (if at all)

comes experience! But surely reflection by its very nature (and as the word implies) comes *second*.

That was a long preamble, but necessary. What does it mean then when a Catholic or a Christian says, My Church, or my religion, is the best? "Our product, our *finished* product, is the best"? It couldn't mean anything as crude as that. But it does mean what it says: my Church is the best. But don't forget for an instant: *it is the language of love*. St Francis de Sales wrote to the nuns of the Congregation he had founded, "You need not believe that your Congregation is the best in the world, only that it is the one you *love* best."

This will surely sound like relativism to anyone who believes that the fundamental language of religion is a subject/object language. Such people imagine they can stand outside all religions (where? on a cloud?) and adjudicate between them. This shows a disbelief in the language of love, and even in the nature of love. *But the language of love is a valid language.* Valid, but very vulnerable. It doesn't stand up well to logical analysis.

The man who says his wife is the most wonderful woman in the world is saying something perfectly valid (if he means it). He has come to that expression by his love, not by a process of elimination. Nor is he bound in consequence to say that all other women in the world are "gravely deficient". In certain moments she may put pressure on him to say just that! But if he is faithful to the nature of love he will resist it; it would be changing the nature of the discourse into something else: an assessment that is almost certain eventually to choke up love with comparisons and jealousy. The full mystery of marital love is revealed to the man through this woman and no other. He was never in a position to assess all the women in the world and declare her the winner. And even if he were to declare her a 'winner' in some sense, it would put her in a very competitive and insecure position. His love is unconditional, it doesn't depend on what others are like.

Likewise. he is not in a position to line up all the religions of the world and adjudicate between them objectively; that would be an attempt to play God. The full mystery of God's love is revealed for a Christian through Jesus. And a Christian's love for him is unconditional. That's the nature of love.

I'm happy that you are immersed in this question. Don't give up. It is a wonderful exploration – dangerous too! Love is an eternal apprenticeship, and we all make many mistakes and say gauche things. But forgiveness too is part of love: love *does* mean having to say you're sorry! You are blessed in having living examples of sanctity before you. In living we are one with what we do; in talking we may well be separate from it. Our Faith is a way of living before it is a way of talking. Christians were known as "followers of the way" before they were known as Christians.

Right-wing Catholics

I pray with a group of five or six people once a week, and I've been finding it a great help to me, especially when things trouble me. I used to feel great peace afterwards. But a few months ago we were joined by a man who never stops preaching at us. It's not preaching really but giving out. He's the only man in the group, and he's always correcting people's prayers and telling us that priests are no longer preaching the gospel. He's a right-wing Catholic and he has ruined what we had going. One of the others said to me I should ignore him, but I don't find it possible. I don't look forward any more to Wednesday evenings, I come away cross and I'm tempted to drop out. But that would be giving into him. The others have the same problem with him. What would you recommend us to do?

You got a live one there! I've met more than a few like him. I would suggest that you tell him quietly and clearly about the effect he is having on your group and that you are not willing to let it continue. If this does not change his behaviour, ask him to leave. If he refuses to leave, disband the group, and then regroup somewhere else. This is just common sense: measured escalation.

From earliest times Christian communities have had to work out ways of dealing with erring members. "If another member of the church sins

against you, go and point out the fault when the two of you are alone"
(Matthew 18:15). 'Sin' is not too strong a word in your situation. It's an
intolerable arrogance to correct someone's prayer. It is different only in
degree from disrupting a Mass or a Baptism or a wedding. To continue
the text from Matthew: "If the member listens to you, you have regained
that one. But if you are not listened to, take one or two others along with
you, so that every word may be confirmed by the evidence of two or three
witnesses. If the member refuses to listen to them, tell it to the church;
and if the offender refuses to listen even to the church, let such a one be
to you as a Gentile and a tax collector."

An early Christian writing called *The Didachè* gave instructions on
how to deal with wandering speakers, some of whom, clearly, were
promoting themselves, not faith in Christ. Such a person, it said, should
be welcomed, but later on "you must test him and find out about him."
If he was subversive, they were to pay no attention to him. He was not
to stay more than a day or two. If he stayed three days he was a fake.
Notice that there was no pussyfooting.

Prayer-groups today are sitting ducks for bullies and control-freaks,
because they are usually made up of people who feel that they always
have to be kind and nice. That difficult member is in clover. You're a
perfect audience. What could suit him better than a group of women
who never challenge him? But you are not in fact being kind to him by
tolerating his behaviour.

A friend of mine told me about her parish priest (in the time of Pius
XII) who said to one of his parishioners, "Isn't it wonderful that the pope
has changed the rule about fasting from midnight before Communion?
Now you only have to fast for three hours!" The man said nothing for a
while, and then he said, "Do you think, Father, that the pope is a steady
man?" There are still people who think they are more Catholic than
the pope. When you hear them out you come to see that what they are
attached to is not the faith but their own opinions. Let's not forget that a
large group of such people, with Archbishop Lefèbvre, went into schism
some years back.

The irony of it is considerable: because they thought themselves more faithful to the Church than others, they separated from the Church.

There's a pathetic sort of Catholic fundamentalism that is not based on the Scriptures but on the penny catechism. And just as scriptural fundamentalists rely on a handful of 'proof texts', so these pick and choose what suits them from the penny catechism. You won't hear them taking to heart what it said, for example, about "rash judgment, calumny, and detraction".

The fundamental problem is ignorance of the faith. "People are just thirsting for the truth, Father!" said a contemplative nun to me, laying her hand on her heart, dimming her eyes, and inclining her head to one side. But I soon discovered what she meant by the truth: a few simplistic definitions, and paranoia about 'New Age'. She is not representative of her kind, thank God, but all over the world there are millions of people clinging to shreds and calling them the truth.

However, there's a positive side. There are more laypeople studying theology now than ever before. There is, for example, a 'distance learning' programme of theology, run from the Priory Institute in Tallaght, Dublin, and it is very heartening. Education alone can drive out fundamentalism. Someone said, "Education is expensive, but it's not as expensive as ignorance!"

Latin or such

Have you any comment to make on the resurgence of Latin in the liturgy, and the new translation of the Mass? How do you honestly feel about it?

I was with a group of people when one of them asked if I intended to say Mass for them in Latin. "No," I replied. "May I ask why not?" she said; "are you unable?" I replied that I was old enough to have said Mass in Latin many times. "Why not, then?" she persisted, "It's a sacred language, isn't it?" That touched a nerve. I said, "No, it is not a sacred language. It was the language of the four soldiers who crucified Jesus. As they hammered metal spikes into his wrists and feet they were chatting in

Latin." Chatting about their pay, probably, and their holidays, and their girlfriends…. No, Latin was never a sacred language.

It is a good language for clarity and precision *of ideas*. No doubt the ancient Romans were able to express their *feelings* in it too, but then it died. (Latin has died three times.) With a vastly diminished vocabulary it became the language of mediaeval theology. It is useful to be able to read mediaeval texts in that language. Strange as this may seem, it is easier to read them in Latin than in translation. This is because of the poverty of their vocabulary. But when this theology is translated into English (a language with an immense vocabulary) it sounds and feels very bloodless indeed. Seminarians raised on this bloodless language became priests preaching homilies that carried no evidence of Incarnation, no feeling, no warmth of flesh and blood.

People who want Mass in Latin will have it. My greater difficulty is with a language that is neither Latin nor English. Translating a text is like shipping goods from one country to another. They should be brought the full distance, not dumped half-way in the sea. Unlike Anglicans, Catholics are fairly new to English in the Liturgy. The translation we had was quite good, but needed repairs in places. It was proper English, even if the collects were sometimes a bit flat. But the new 'translation' is a vast disimprovement. It is an invented language, spoken or written by nobody in the world. What can you do, for example, with a phrase like "the venerable exercises of holy devotion"? What kind of chimerical world does that language attempt to put you into? I find it hard to see anything to like in this new 'translation' of the missal. It does change 'everlasting' to 'eternal' in one place – which is an improvement – but then it does not do so consistently. Linguists would not describe it as a translation at all, but as a *relexification*: that is, an artificial language created by inserting the vocabulary of one language into the structures of another.

The danger is that it will only increase the feeling of vertigo that most Catholics experience at present. When we are being swept into a hurricane of change by events in the Church and in the world around us, we would have liked the Liturgy to remain as it has been for the last four decades. But now everything is in a spin. Perhaps the idea was to give us a 'timeless' Liturgy, one that disdained the passing fashions of the world. They should have reflected on Ronald Knox's translation of the Bible, likewise intended to be timeless, but now utterly dated and unusable.

An old priest says the texts are "unspeakable", a choir-master says they are "unsingable", lacking all rhythm. Why then are we burdened with them? It appears now that the imposition of this botched 'translation' was an exercise in power; it was to teach the English-speaking world a lesson; it was to bury the Vatican II doctrine of the collegiality of bishops. In 1998 the eleven English-speaking hierarchies of the world produced a splendid translation of the missal, the fruit of fifteen years of scholarly labour. (You can find it on the internet.) This work was brushed aside by the Chilean Cardinal Medina Estévez, Prefect of the Congregation for Divine Worship and the Discipline of the Sacraments – who knew no English! In its place we have this ugly hybrid.

The most striking change – because the most prominently placed – is the substitution of "many" for "all" in the words of consecration. The Italian hierarchy voted unanimously to reject this change in their liturgy: from *per tutti* (for all) to *per molti* (for many), and the Vatican accepted this. St Paul wrote explicitly that "Christ died for all" (2 Corinthians 5:14-15), so there can be no question of scaling back the redemption. In English we are now left to explain to people that "many" really means "all".

Using this 'translation' is like driving on a badly pot-holed road. Instead of uniformity, it will produce endless diversity as celebrants swerve to avoid the worst potholes. We must just keep our fingers crossed and hope that this new 'translation' will not be too great a distraction or an irritant for congregations. One thing is guaranteed: every day will be a field-day for liturgical spies. They are already beginning to show their faces on the internet.

As you see, I can offer you no joy here. Hope? Well, in the end the Liturgy is an action and not only a set of readings. What makes the biggest difference is the *way* it is celebrated. We all have our wish-lists. Mine would be for a liturgical speed-limit, and mandatory pauses – a more prayerful and contemplative experience. Now that this new 'translation' is a done deed, let's pray that it will not do enormous damage to the Eucharist, this supersensitive nerve-centre of our faith.

— 3 —
Spirituality

Repent and believe what?

I look at a lot of Christian stuff on the net and I'm surprised at the immense variety. I mean some of it is all fire and brimstone, and more of it is the very opposite. Is it the same Jesus they're talking about? Which of them is right, or are they all making it up? Please throw some light on this.

It is true to some extent that we all invent our own Jesus. But that is not so surprising. In a way we all invent our own world. Two people look at the same landscape: one loves it, the other hates it or is bored by it. Two people watch some event, and their accounts of it are entirely different. What we like and dislike says much about ourselves; sometimes it says more about ourselves than about anything else.

Is there anything true then, you ask; is everything just opinion? No. I think the fact that we *argue* about something shows that we still believe that truth is possible. Picture two people arguing, even bitterly, about something: they are far nearer to each other than two others who just shrug their shoulders. What looks like total disagreement is never quite that.

Yes, we hear many different versions of the Gospel, and we are presented with many different kinds of Jesus. We are often asked to believe in a Jesus who belongs more in the Old Testament than in the New. Many fundamentalist Christians, it seems to me, are far more at home in the Old Testament. We all hope that we are on a route (with many stages, and a slightly different Jesus at each stage) that will lead us to the real Jesus.

Many sermons present us with John the Baptist rather than Jesus.

Repent and believe the bad news.

Compare John with Jesus as they first appear in the New Testament. John said the most awful things to people: he called them "a brood of vipers," and he said they deserved nothing but destruction. He came from the desert, where "he wore a garment made of camel-hair … and his food was locusts and wild honey" (Matthew 3:4). His message was equally rough. He didn't begin, "My dear brothers and sisters." He began, "Brood of vipers …!" (Luke 3:7). People wondered if was the Messiah, the Promised One. Many thought he might be. This shows that they had no glamorised image of the Messiah. They expected a thrashing. God would burn up most of them like chaff, John promised. This was a significant phrase, because the Pharisees used to say that the common people were chaff – empty husks. And still the people flocked to hear him. How is that? *He must have been playing by accepted rules.* Criticism is acceptable if it doesn't come too close. John was their theatre; he was the horror movie of his time; he was even dressed for the part. Parish missions with fire and brimstone, even in my lifetime, were greatly enjoyed by all. There was no TV then. John was pure theatre.

Jesus came from the desert too, but he was much friendlier. He sat down to table with all kinds of people whom the locals would call scum. He spoke of mercy and forgiveness and hope. He said that prostitutes would enter the Kingdom of heaven ahead of the pious (Matthew 21:31); he praised the faith of people of other religions and none: Samaritans, Roman centurions, the Syro-Phoenician woman…. This was clearly breaking the rules. They wanted their theatre (as we all do) to be safely 'out there': they went "out" to John the Baptist (Luke 7:26). But Jesus came in; he saw them from the inside; he didn't "play the prophet," as he was challenged to do (Luke 22:64). He believed in them; he said of them, "The harvest is rich but the labourers are few …" (Matthew 9:36): in other words, he didn't see them as chaff (as the Pharisees did) but as harvest – ripe and full of life. He respected them; but because he got into their minds and saw what they were made of, they rejected him. He knew them too well; if their illusions were to live on, he had to die.

It is strange: John was distant and scolding, and they accepted him. It is clear that he loved people less; he preferred to put the fear of God into them. Jesus was close and friendly and he was rejected. People are strange.

"Who are you?" the people asked John. "How do you see yourself?" Today we tend to turn the searchlight inwards. "Who am I?" "How do I see myself?" In our complex world these are not trivial questions. There are many who are willing to offer us ready-made identities. Some of these identities are intensely tight-fitting: the world is full of cults and fanatical movements, secular and religious. Many look at you and don't want to know who you are; they see only the identity they would like to impose on you. We need to escape from false identities – our own and other people's egos – and keep looking for our real identity in Christ.

But who is Christ? "Among you stands one whom you do not know," said John, referring to Christ. We do not know him because we cannot get away forever with imposing an identity on him, though we try all the time: Jesus the Catholic, Jesus the Protestant, Jesus the Baptist.... But the truth keeps setting him free.

He said to us, "The truth will set you free." The ego has a drowning man's grip. We have to set Jesus free if he is to save us. The test is whether that is actually working for us. Are we in fact being set free? He said, "Love one another as I have loved you." Can we detect any signs of it? If we can we are on the right path.

Vatican document on New Age

I'm very worried about my husband who is a recovering alcoholic. He's off the drink for four years now and he attends his AA meetings every Wednesday and Saturday. He was drinking heavily when I married him and we had a terrible life for nearly ten years – I won't go into it. It's great to have enough money now for decent clothes and proper food....

I read in a magazine that the Church has condemned AA. Is that true? If it is I can't understand it. Our life would still be hell only for it. I'm terrified that my husband will find out it's condemned and go back on the drink. He's very religious. How can it be wrong when it does so much good for people?

Can you tell me something about that document?

The magazine was referring, no doubt, to a 2003 document from two Vatican bodies, the Pontifical Council for Culture and the Pontifical Council for Inter-Religious Dialogue, entitled *Jesus Christ, the Bearer of the Water of Life – a Christian Reflection on the 'New Age'*. No, I can tell you straight away, it is not true that the document condemns AA or any of the twelve-step programmes such as Narcotics Anonymous or Gamblers Anonymous. Notice that the document calls itself a "reflection", not a judgment or a condemnation. Thank God for that – for it would be difficult to name any movement that has been even half as effective as these twelve-step programmes in helping people who are struggling with addictions.

The one and only reference to these programmes is in a section entitled "Health: Golden Living", where it gives a list of about 25 so-called 'New Age' approaches to promoting holistic health. It includes the twelve-step programmes in that list. Attempting to describe these approaches, the document says, "The source of healing is said to be within ourselves, something we reach when we are in touch with our inner energy or cosmic energy" (2.2.3). Elsewhere the document says that New Age thinking involves the "rejection of the language of sin and salvation, replacing it with the morally neutral language of addiction and recovery" (2.4).

If I could make just two points about this:

1. I doubt that any AA or Al Anon member could see in these phrases anything resembling their own or their family member's struggle for recovery. From listening to hundreds of AA members over many years I can say that what impresses me continually is their deep understanding of the need to hand over their lives daily to the 'Higher Power'. They come on their knees begging God for help. (The phrase 'Higher Power', rather than 'God', was adopted by the founders of AA, not because they were vague about their faith, but because they wanted non-believers too to come to recovery.)

2. Alcoholics, like all addicts, are nearly always crippled with guilt; they have no doubt at all about being sinners. They come to AA precisely

because all their own moralising – and that of others – has failed to help them. In AA they begin to learn that there is not a simple equation between sinner and addict (even though all human beings are sinners); they begin to understand the nature of addiction and they begin to find some glimmer of hope for recovery. Many do recover. This is a way that works. It begins where preaching has failed.

All the themes of the AA and similar programmes are deeply spiritual, as anyone can see from reading the Twelve Steps. So, rest assured that AA is not condemned in this document. It is a pity that the document referred to the twelve-step programmes at all.

You asked for further comments on the document itself. This document tries to get a handle on the New Age movement as such. It has to admit of course that this is less a movement than a cultural climate with very unclear boundaries. "The mere use of the term New Age in itself means little, if anything" (6.2), it says, and some things "are frequently labelled 'New Age' for commercial purposes" (1.4).

Having said that, it goes on, surprisingly, to speak of it as if it did indeed mean one thing: "The gnostic nature of this movement calls us to judge it in its entirety" (4). No dialogue here, only an array of answers! It calls itself "a provisional report", and "an invitation to understand the New Age and to engage in a genuine dialogue with those who are influenced by New Age thought" (1); it "does not aim at providing a set of complete answers to the many questions raised by the New Age" (1). Yet by pasting onto it the names of ancient heresies – 'Gnosticism' (second century), 'Pelagianism' (fourth century), 'Quietism' (seventeenth century) – it does indeed prejudice the case; name-calling is hardly a form of dialogue.

Neither is it analysis. To say 'A is like B' is not to analyse A, because A is also in fact unlike B (inescapably so when A is twenty-first century and B is second century). It admits that "the term New Age has even been abused to demonise people and practices" (6.2). The document itself, despite its own disclaimers, has many passages that are examples of just that. It is written in a new style – almost chatty. It doesn't quite come off, however. It appears gauche, probably because it is so new, and the old style lies just below the surface. For example, "this is very much an 'either-or' situation" (6.1) is a reasonable translation of *anathema sit!* There are many similar examples.

I think there is no substitute for going into each of the practices alluded to by the woolly term 'New Age', and doing so *painstakingly, one by one*. When 25 practices are put in the same bag with things like Satanism and sorcery, everything in the bag is soiled. This is not the way to understand anything. In the thirteenth century the philosophy of Aristotle, as it came to the West in the translations of Islamic scholars, must have appeared to most Christians as a "deterministic" system – in that respect a little like "Aquarian thinking". While some people went along with it uncritically, others condemned it out of hand, and others again went along happily with both (a position known as *duplex veritas* – 'double truth'), St Albert the Great and St Thomas Aquinas set themselves the much more laborious task of studying it in depth and painstakingly integrating much of it into Christian theology. There is no substitute for that painstaking labour.

The situation is also like (and unlike!) that at the beginning of the twentieth century. Then too the Church, under Pius X, had to take account of a new climate of thought. It named it 'Modernism', summarised it, formulated it in its own way, and condemned it with extreme violence of language, initiating what has been called "a Reign of Terror in the Church" that lasted 50 years. The present reaction, thank God, is very different. The manner (thinly-veiled mockery) pretends at least to be friendly, more humble, sometimes tentative; and the word 'dialogue' is used even if there is no real evidence of it.

I pray that your husband will continue with AA, which has already brought such blessings to your family and such hope to so many around the world.

New Age influence on Christian spirituality

I was at a meditation meeting lately and I was listening to someone talking about meditation. It was in a retreat house and I assumed that it would be about Christian meditation, but there was not much mention of Christ or anything you could call religious. He talked about depth and stillness and so on. He always began with a prayer, but after that I could not be sure of it. There is a lot of this going on now, and I am just asking for some clarification, I suppose. Someone told me about a Buddhist giving talks on meditation to Catholics. How could people like that know anything about the Christian faith?

My short answer is: Don't judge the book by the cover. There's a passage in Matthew's gospel that speaks to this. "Not everyone who says to me, 'Lord, Lord,' will enter the kingdom of heaven, but only the one who does the will of my Father in heaven" (7:21; also Luke 6:36). There are people who never stop talking about Jesus but have none of his spirit, just as there are people who seldom mention him but are filled with his spirit. We put a heavy emphasis on *words* – perhaps too heavy.

In that retreat house, no doubt, everything proclaimed that this was Christian meditation. The pictures on the wall, the timetable, the meals, the people there: everything was saying "This is done in the name of Jesus." Why should they have to keep on saying it over and over in words as well? "If the walls could talk …" we say. But they do, they do. And what a relief that they do! Places, rooms, contexts, pictures, gestures…. everything is a language – a language, but not speech. We're living in one of the most talkative cultures the world has seen: newspapers, magazines, radio, TV, the internet, mobile phones… all piling up tidal waves of *words* that wash over us. In this deluge of words the Word is going unheard. Is it any wonder that people want to be silent? No doubt there are Christians who are unsure of what they believe, but I know that many go for meditation in order to hear the Word. I don't know anyone who goes in order to exclude Christ.

I doubt very much that a Buddhist was just giving talks on meditation. They prefer to do it rather than talk about it. I've never heard of any who just talk about it. Christians are the ones who are more likely to do that.

Now I want to ask you a question. If what Christians affirm is really true, and not just an attitude or a way of looking – a 'blik', as an English philosopher once called it – then would you not expect it to be visible to others in some way? Imperfectly, perhaps, but visible in principle? If a tree is really out there in the garden, and not just in your mind, would you be surprised that your neighbour could see it too? He sees it from a different angle, it may have a different significance for him, and he may not love it as you do, but it is not invisible to him. You have to be careful when you stress the special nature of Christian faith that you are not diminishing its truth claim. Jesus praised the "faith" of a Roman centurion, who was a pagan. "Truly I tell you, in no one in Israel have I found such faith" (Matthew 8:10). This ought to make us reflect deeply on what we mean by faith. Clearly it must mean much more than a badge of identity. That Roman pagan was not a member of the community of faith. In fact Jesus himself was regarded as an outsider and a blasphemer.

It is true that we have to "test the spirits to see whether they are from God" (1 John 4:1), but we shouldn't be tempted to think we know in advance what the result will be.

Catholic New Age

Do you believe in apparitions of Our Lady and messages and images of Mary appearing on walls and tree-stumps…? Something you said last month makes me think you don't. But I would like to hear more from you about it…. There's a book of messages from our Lady to a north-side Dublin woman; a neighbour keeps telling me I should buy it. I notice she doesn't offer to make me a present of it! The way to read it, she said, is to open it at random and there's your message. Is all this stuff ok or is it slightly mad?

I'm not tempted to believe in any of that. But it is of great interest, all the same. If you were tempted to throw around the vague term 'New Age', you could call it New Age for traditional Catholics. It is a religion of the senses: it has the appeal of the tangible and the immediate, yet far from being incarnational it is other-worldly in the extreme; it bypasses reflection, and it bypasses community; it is a thirst for signs and wonders.

Thanks for the word 'mojo' in the part of your letter I omitted here. I looked it up. Yes, I agree that the Church has lost its magic touch, its mojo. People have been bored just too often by homilies that have no content or interest, by slip-shod liturgies, and by being excluded from parish life or not invited into it. And just for these reasons they look elsewhere. They would prefer that it wasn't 'elsewhere', so they create their own mojo within the familiar coordinates. In the 1980s it was all about 'moving statues'. At one point this became so widespread that some people were watching statues to see if they would move. Then suddenly all the statues stopped moving. Nobody asked what set them moving, and nobody asked what made them stop. But the search for mojo goes on.

Messages from Our Lady are a kind of "channelling." I was startled to hear someone read "messages from Our Lady" from the lectern where the Gospel had just been proclaimed at Mass. The effect was to say that the Gospel was a thing of the past – because these 'messages' were from yesterday or just this morning.

If people had any historical awareness, or if they retained a vestige of good sense, they would see that all this happened many times before and it is situated near the lunatic end of the spectrum. Useful background reading would be Ronald Knox's 1950 book *Enthusiasm*. Enthusiasm tends to sweep everything away, as these modern enthusiasts are willing to sweep the Church's experience away. "May God forgive him," announced a recent enthusiast when a bishop cast doubt on his prediction that Mary was going to appear at Knock on a precise date, at 3 pm. Thousands of people had turned up for the event; but strangely, only the enthusiast himself claimed that it took place – even though everybody was watching. A priest in Medjugorge complained bitterly that people were talking in church; and sure enough, there was a 'message from Our Lady' next morning to say that "people should remain silent in my Son's church." What can you do when people lose their good sense?

The demand for miracles and wonders is the *mysticism of extraverts*. Everything has to be 'out there': apparitions, messages, strange occurrences and coincidences…. Where there is no inner enlightenment you have external visions. Highly rational people – at one in this with very simple people – are the most readily convinced by these. This is puzzling until you hit the key word: *extravert*. For a highly rational person a 'miracle' is new data in the lab. It was the highly rationalistic theologies that depended most heavily on them. Meanwhile there is a whole world untouched: the ego world of self-deception, projection, wishful thinking.... But that is outside the frame of rationality, so it is not acknowledged: it is not 'objective', so it is merely 'irrational'. When it is acknowledged at all, it is seen only as *wilful* self-deception. To call it wilful is the way to dismiss it. In reality it is far more potent when it is not wilful. But that is a place the extravert person does not want to go.

This appetite for signs and wonders is not a new thing. "The Pharisees came and began to argue with Jesus, asking him for a sign from heaven, to test him. And he sighed deeply in his spirit and said, 'Why does this generation ask for a sign? Truly I tell you, no sign will be given to this generation.'" (Mk 8:11).

Eastern spirituality

I'd like to hear your views on eastern spirituality. There seems to be a lot of it around these times in bookshops and workshops and everywhere you look, and I've heard different views on it. I've heard it called a threat to Christianity, but if it is, why can you find it in Catholic bookshops and retreat houses? In other words, is it as good or as bad as it's cracked up to be?

Thanks for your letter and your wide-open question. It leaves me with a lot of choice on how to reply.

The first point I'd like to make is this: Christianity itself is an Eastern religion. But to approach your question from that side would take us into questions you are not asking. I'll just refer you to an introductory book on that subject, *The Spirituality of the Christian East: A Systematic Handbook*, by Tomáš Špidlík.

What you are asking about, I think, is Eastern non-Christian religions, such as Buddhism, Taoism, Hinduism....

We know more about our neighbours now than ever before. The sacred books of all the world religions, along with shelves of commentary, are available in bookshops almost everywhere, as you noticed, and on the internet. This must be very bewildering for many people, giving the appearance of a religious supermarket; and the 'local shops', so to speak, don't like it. A Catholic journalist recently headed his piece "Spirituality: Religion without the Effort". But such reactions, while revealing a great deal about the writer, say nothing at all sensible about spirituality, either Christian or non-Christian. These neighbours are here to stay. Call them immigrants if you wish. Here they may appear to be fringe elements, but at home they are part of an ancient culture.

From the beginning, Christianity has borrowed massively from other sources. This is another vast subject, and again I will refer you to a very accessible book, *The Study of Spirituality* (edited by C. Jones, G. Wainwright and E. Arnold, SPCK 1986). Take just two instances. Referring to the work of the Greek philosopher Plato (428 BC–347 BC), one of the contributors, Anthony Meredith, writes, "It is impossible to exaggerate the influence of such language on all the Christian mystical tradition from Origen [born 185 AD] onwards." It would be equally hard to exaggerate the influence of Aristotle (384 BC–22 BC), famously on St Albert the Great and St Thomas Aquinas. But here, it may be, lies the key. Ultimately it may require saints and scholars of their stature – or something like it – to make profound dialogue with these religions.

The Christian dialogue with Buddhism and other Oriental religions is in its early stages, but it has begun. It is interesting that it is through monasticism on both sides that the most promising advances are being made. See for example the *Bulletin of the Monastic Interreligious Dialogue Commissions*. If religions are to move closer and talk to one another, it must be through their most contemplative voices.

It is easy to notice lines of convergence and even similarities of expression, but this is just the beginning of an acquaintance. It is like meeting some strangers and finding to your delight that you can understand a few words of their speech. There is a long way to go before they become your soul-mates. There is the danger of syncretism, of course. The Dalai Lama often refers humorously to people's attempts "to put a yak's head on an ox." It seems to be a universal rule that when you try to make two groups of people into one, you end up with three groups. There is the new 'unity' group, and there will always be people on both sides who refuse to move: that makes three. I think there can never be a question of unifying even Christian denominations in that way, let alone world religions. It is not a question of merging; initially it is not even about agreement. It is not so much about unity of mind as unity of heart: mutual respect and appreciation. Without these there is no way forward.

When I meet a real stranger I find out new things about myself. Someone said that Buddhists are the first real strangers Christians have had to talk with. They can show us our blind spots (even without intending to) precisely because they are strangers. Many Christians discover depths *in their own religion* through contact with Buddhism and other religions.

But some rush in blindly. When Western people abandon Christianity and embrace a non-Christian religion, they cut their own spiritual roots and leave themselves vulnerable to being lost between two worlds. What they get from the Oriental religion is what a Western person can get, which may not be what the Oriental religion has to give. (I still remember an American saying to a group of us, many years ago, "You with your Western mentality….")

As for superficial borrowing: I'm reminded of the story of the actress who invited George Bernard Shaw to marry her, "Our children would have my looks and your brains." Shaw replied, "But what if they had my looks and your brains?" There is no guarantee, when it comes to mixing anything, that we will get the best of both. It's an even chance that we will get the worst of both. In matters religious the chances may be considerably less than even.

A religion is a deep and subtle mystery, and only its great mystics get to the bottom of it – but they are the very ones who say they know nothing. The rest of us, not knowing that depth, will look for similarities. But if we are forever looking for *similarities* we will eventually live in a very boring world – and that's the worst of both.

Eastern religions and God

I saw a programme on religions and it seems there is no God in Buddhism but hundreds of them in Hinduism. The Christian Creed says, "We believe in one God." What are we to say? Is our belief in one God better than belief in none, and not as good as a belief in hundreds!

The number of deities in Hinduism is said to be 33 crores. A crore is 10 million. Obviously the word 'deity' or 'god' in that context doesn't mean what Christians mean by it. Hinduism is better seen as a family of religions than as a single religion. It embraces a great variety of doctrines, cults, and ways of life; and the worship of local gods does not exclude belief in a single high God. Local gods are also seen as manifestations of a high God. It is said that no religious idea in India ever dies or is superseded; it is just combined with the rest. Hindus are inclined to revere the divine in everything.

This sounds alien to a Christian mind, but then many of the things we forget or never knew about our own religion sound almost as alien. For example, St Thomas Aquinas could write, "God is one in reality but multiple according to our minds; we know him in as many ways as created things represent him." This is not to imagine that the Hinduism and Christianity could be 'synchronised' in some way – why would anyone be tempted to do such a thing? At present, the best we can do with other religions is to realise we don't understand them, to have the grace to respect them, and perhaps to learn through them how little we have plumbed the depths of our own.

Buddhists were gravely offended some years ago when Pope John Paul II described their religion as "atheistic". The Buddha was a Hindu of the fifth century BC. When questioned about God *he remained silent*.

He neither affirmed nor denied the existence of a God or crores of gods. He refused to be drawn into the jungle of speculation. His silence was his answer. Was that atheism? One might as well call St Thomas Aquinas an atheist, who said, "Neither Christian nor pagan knows the nature of God as he is in himself," and who gave up writing because, he said, "all I have written is just straw compared to what have been revealed to me." Or Meister Eckhart, who said, "God, who has no name; God is ineffable."

This is not to pretend to capture the two religions in one view, but it is to see at the very least that the other religion is worthy of respect and consideration. This is the very least we owe one another. There are about 300 million Buddhists in the world today. They were given even greater offence when a very prominent cardinal in an interview with the French magazine *L'Express* in 1997 described their religion as "a form of spiritual auto-eroticism." It beggars belief that anyone, let alone a Christian so prominently placed, should utter these degrading words.

Please don't repeat that Buddhists are atheists. It doesn't describe them; it doesn't describe the way they live; it doesn't even describe the way they talk. Jesus praised the faith of people of other religions and none: Samaritans, Roman centurions, the Syro-Phoenician woman.... And he said, "Not everyone who says to me, 'Lord, Lord,' will enter the kingdom of heaven, but only the one who does the will of my Father in heaven" (Matthew 7:21).

Christians inherit "the one only God" of the Old Testament, marking us off from Hindus and Buddhists alike. But that God is changed in the process – something we don't always sufficiently acknowledge. For example, there's a passage in the Old Testament that Christians especially love to quote. It is about "God in the gentle breeze". That passage is about the prophet Elijah's encounter with God. "There was a great wind ... but God was not in the wind; and after the wind an earthquake, but God was not in the earthquake; and after the earthquake a fire, but God was not in the fire; and after the fire a sound of a gentle breeze" (1 Kings 19:11-12). In another translation it is even nicer: instead of the gentle breeze there is "sheer silence" (NRSV). Other translations say, "a still small voice," or "the sound of a soft breath," or "a quiet whispering voice." All this would seem to make us think of the God of the Old Testament as a soft, gentle, unchallenging Presence – until we read on and hear what was said to Elijah in that 'soft whispering voice'; God told him take up his sword and put his enemies to death!

You could say that we Christians misread this text – and many others. We take it out of context and apply it wholesale. But we have always been doing this with the Old Testament.

The biggest alteration to the one God of Judaism is of course the Christian teaching on the Trinity of Persons. But that is a long story. The full scope of Christian revelation is vast. It is as vast as three religions! You can't miss God. No matter which way you point (up to the Father, out and around you to Jesus, and in to the Spirit) you get caught up in the vast net.

Christianity is able to feel with all the religions of the world, because it has something of them in itself. Of course Christians have often ignored or despised them in the course of its history, but that is not the spirit of Christianity. We are to discern the spirits, to see which come from God. The spirit of our Faith is as wide as the world – wider than the world.

Vipassana

I would normally move away from Roman Catholic stuff'! I was brought up very strict RC and eventually found solace in the Vipassana meditation. Having explored lots and been open to all, I have often thought that we need to not stay stuck in the intricacies of specific doctrines. Rather to take the core precepts from all and make that Big Blancmange that you seemed to recoil from!!? You said something like, "Oh no, we don't want that big blancmange. We know what we mean." I don't know what you mean. Why, please tell me, do we need to stay adhered to one 'club'? Is it to do with fearing loss of identity? Isn't that the point?

I remember an old man in hospital, years ago, who kept producing a photo of his wife, talking about her to everyone and saying, "Why did she marry me?" When I enquired, he told me she was dead for 19 years. He had no answer to his question, nor did he want an answer. If someone were to give him an answer in financial or social terms or the like, he would reject it instantly. He wanted to stay with his question because it was a question about love.

To judge by our performance, religion, sadly, is often about hatred and a tribal spirit; but it is meant to be about love. It is love alone that raises it above sectarianism. In the earliest days of the Christian faith, some members of the Pharisee sect had become followers of Jesus, and they wanted to bring their practices with them (Acts 15:5).

They were thwarted then, but they have had many successors over the centuries. There are many Catholics who have the words of Christ on their lips but not his spirit of love in their hearts. The status before God of such persons should be a much more agonising question for Catholics than the status of non-Catholics and non-Christians. Everything comes back to one astonishing brief sentence: "Whoever does not love does not know God, for God is love" (1 John 4:8). When there is no love there is no knowledge of God, and it is then that all the tribalism and all the brazen assertions of identity flood in to fill the vacuum.

Love is a great paradox: it is a perfectly general force, but it is in love with the particular. A man falls in love with a particular woman, not all women. He may be attracted to very many of them, but he is really in love with only one. He doesn't really mind if other people fail to understand his choice or fail to find that woman beautiful. If he tells her she is the most beautiful woman in the world, they both know that he is not a disinterested judge; what he is expressing is his love, not the results of a beauty contest. His declaration of love, though it appears subjective, has a deeper truth in it than the result of any beauty contest. The beauty contest may appear objective, but is it? And even if physical beauty were measurable, such a thing is very shallow compared to the so-called 'subjective' choice of a person in love. Shunryu Suzuki suggests in *Zen Mind, Beginner's Mind*:

When you understand one thing through and through, you understand everything. When you try to understand everything, you will not understand anything.

I think it makes more sense to think of religion in this way, rather than as membership of a 'club'. Our initial choice of metaphor will shape everything we go on to say about religion. Membership of a club is a rather passionless affair, but love is a passion. If there's no passion everything is equal because everything is neutral and boring. Then the only recourse is to pick out a few bits that are not as bad as the rest, add them to some bits from other religions, and there's your blancmange! But a passionate attachment to one religion by no means prevents a person from appreciating the depth of another religion. On the contrary I think it helps. A man who is incapable of loving one woman is incapable of loving any woman. The genius of the Christian faith is its concreteness: the Incarnation, the Eucharist, all the sacraments, all its rituals.

I'm glad to hear that you have found something you are passionate about in Vipassana. Anyone who has ever practised Vipassana or followed a Zen *sesshin* will know that this is not an easy option. The prospect of 10 hours (or more) of meditation a day would frighten the wits out of most people. I have sat many *sesshin* myself and I know how challenging they are. I couldn't imagine for a moment that the smallest part of that work and goodwill is wasted, no matter who does it. The normal path for a Catholic is the Catholic faith, but God is not restricted to what we call normal. "God is greater than our hearts," St John said; and St Paul said, "No one comprehends what is truly God's except the Spirit of God" (1 Corinthians 2:11).

I read the sacred books of many religions and I learn something very precious from them – sometimes just because their angle of view is different. It was through Zen that I discovered Meister Eckhart, for example, even though I am a member of the same religious Order as he! I don't think Catholics have to put their own faith between brackets in order to study other religions. It often happens that they discover something of their own faith by seeing it through different eyes. No need to pick and choose. If there are parts of my faith that I am unable to fathom at present, there is no need to deny their meaning or value; just let me be patient. God is greater than my heart and mind.

Zen

You frequently mention Zen Buddhism in your website and in your articles. I'm wondering how this finds a place in Catholic circles. I can't say it's un-orthodox Christianity, because it's not Christian at all. Can you not supply Catholic material without reaching for exotic things like Zen? What can it mean to ordinary people? I'm sure you have your reasons, but I'd like to hear you elaborate on them.

I have heard more than one Zen master declare that Zen is not a religion. It arose within Buddhism, but it is not confined within Buddhism. The word 'zen' means *meditation*, and meditation is for people of any and every religious persuasion. Meditation is part of Catholic tradition too, of course. It is part of every serious religious tradition. To ask which religion it belongs to is like asking which country water comes from. It belongs everywhere. There are now several Zen masters in the world who are Catholic – including Catholic priests and Sisters and lay people.

Why bother at all with Zen if meditation is part of Catholic tradition? The reason is that Zen is utterly clear and rigorous and practical about it, while some (not all) Catholic sources can be quite diffuse and wordy – more aspirational than practical. When I quote Zen masters and writers it is because they are saying exactly what I as a Catholic want to say, but they are saying it better than I could. They are not saying everything I want to say, but when our interests overlap, their practical approach is clearly better.

Is meditation 'neutral', then, from a religious point of view? Yes. Meditation in itself is just meditation, just as water is water. But when a Christian meditates, it is a Christian activity. When a Christian breathes, that is a Christian activity. We make meditation Christian by being Christians. A Buddhist makes it Buddhist by being Buddhist.

A twelfth-century Carthusian monk named Guigo expounded a

four-step path of prayer: *lectio, meditatio, oratio, contemplatio. Lectio* was slow prayerful reading of the Scriptures; *meditatio* meant turning over in the mind what one had read; *oratio* meant turning this to conversation with God; and *contemplatio* meant a silent resting in the presence of God. The usage has changed in modern times. When people speak about 'meditation' nowadays they don't mean what Christians meant traditionally by *meditatio*; they mean something much closer to what we meant by *contemplatio*. By and large, Christians have gone along with this change in words. There are countless groups of Christians throughout the world who meet on a weekly basis for what is now called 'meditation', and who practise it daily at home. This is one of the truly great developments in our time. It is a kind of silent revolution: you won't read about it in the papers.

When you join such a group you discover that meditation is not as easy as it might seem. What could be less demanding, we might think, than to sit in silence for half an hour? But we soon realise that it is quite difficult, because the mind is restless. It is a major challenge to quieten it. This is where the practical experience and wisdom of Zen is of immense help. It is not an attempt to substitute one's Christian spirituality for Buddhist, but rather to pacify the mind so that it can truly be present to God, and not just to its own endless chatter. We need all the help we can get.

A visitor to our retreat centre here in Tallaght remarked recently that she was unhappy to see that many of the pictures on the walls were nature scenes; she would have preferred "something more Catholic". What is Catholic? The word itself means 'universal'. Numerous Catholic mystics have stressed that "*every creature* is a word of God." St Bonaventure said that creation is God's first book. Every creature is trying to express God to the best of its ability. Meister Eckhart put it in his characteristically striking way: "Every creature is trying to be Jesus." Jesus is the full revelation of God in human reality, but every creature is doing its best to reveal God. The sea in that picture in the dining room is a revelation of God! All the trees and plants in those pictures are Catholics, if you want to put it that way. And the plants in the window-boxes are devout

Catholics…! Still, I did a quick check after she left, and I found that of the 109 pictures in the entire centre, just 21 were nature scenes. God's first book is, if anything, under-represented.

I hope these few lines will help to put the Catholic interest in Zen in context, Frances. If you want to read further you could pick up *Zen Gifts to Christians* and *Zen Mind, Catholic Mind* by Robert Kennedy SJ. He is a Catholic priest and also a Zen master.

Jon Kabat-Zinn

I've been reading the books of Jon Kabat-Zinn on mindfulness meditation with great interest. I've struggled with my own meditation practice over the years and Kabat-Zinn draws on the whole Buddhist tradition to present a practical western form of meditation that people can use to cope with the stress and strains of modern everyday living. These books … advise concentration on the Breath alone. I've capitalised the word 'breath' because very often when I'm meditating, as a Christian, I find myself chuckling at my puny efforts to concentrate on the literal breath when it is, in fact, highly symbolic of the great cosmic Mystery…. Kabat-Zinn uses the expressions "consciousness discipline" and "spiritual practice" because of the negative connotations associated with religion historically and currently. This is probably me being "too much in my head" over words, but I felt I had to write just to try and clarify my mind a little.

Yes, I've read a couple of Jon Kabat-Zinn's books. When someone of his academic standing (PhD in molecular biology from MIT, Professor of Medicine emeritus at the University of Massachusetts Medical School) brings meditation into the mainstream of medicine, we know we are in an age of convergence, a time of exceptional interest, perhaps especially for religious people: since the very word 'religion', some say, comes from '*religare*', 'to bond, or bind into one'. His work is to teach people mindfulness – for its own sake, of course, but also as a way to help patients cope with pain, sickness and stress.

It is true that his idiom has a Buddhist flavour, but most of what he writes is just plain common sense. He studied with the Korean Zen Master Seung Sahn, and is obviously widely read in Zen literature. "Why does everything related to mindfulness have to be connected to Buddhism?" someone asked. Someone else called it "the B-word", as if it were something indecent.

I was once at a Christian-Zen retreat where there was a daily question-and-answer session. The person who had distinguished himself for sleeping during the meditation periods (and even during the daily talk by the Zen master), woke up one day and asked in a rather accusing tone, "Do you people believe in the next life?" There he was, enquiring about the next life and sleeping his way through this one! I'm afraid many of us do the same thing, perhaps just a little less blatantly. We should be grateful to anyone, whether Christian or Buddhist, who encourages us to wake up and come to our senses. As it happens, Kabat-Zinn has a book with that very title: *Coming to Our Senses*.

Does meditation (or mindfulness) take us out of a Christian orbit and into a Buddhist one? A Zen master responded to this question by saying that Zen is not a religion; it originated in Buddhism but it is not tied to it. There are now several Zen masters who are Catholics, many of them priests and nuns. What they find in Zen is what had been left lying largely neglected in the Christian tradition. It is often through looking at other traditions that we see things neglected in our own. It does not require a giant leap of insight to see this: we experience it all the time in daily life; through our relationships with other people we understand ourselves better. Christianity is not a narrow self-regarding sect. Christians can be at home in the Christian world because we can look out from it and see the entire spectrum. Otherwise it would not be a world, would it?

You mention your "puny efforts to concentrate on the literal breath." It's easy in itself to "ride the waves of the breath," as Kabat-Zinn puts it, but it's not easy to keep it up. When we give ourselves to this practice, however, we begin to be a little free of the collective Attention Deficit Disorder that our society suffers from. It is then that we have some chance of sensing the "great cosmic Mystery," as you called it. The breath is not a trivial thing; it is the doorway to this awareness. Certainly, Christians see great symbolism in the breath. God "breathed the breath of life" into Adam (Genesis 2:7); Jesus breathed on the disciples, saying "Receive the Holy Spirit [the Breath]" (John 20:22). But we enter deeply into this mystery by doing it, not by thinking about it. Thinking is a good thing in itself, but it is no substitute for the reality – just as thinking about food will not nourish you but only make you hungrier. Or it is like drinking seawater. Thinking goes on forever; left to itself, it allows no room for any other kind of awareness. This is why we concentrate on the breath, an activity that (from the point of view of thinking) seems like 'degree zero'. But we have to do this to make room for something other than thinking.

You mentioned Kabat-Zinn's use of the expressions "consciousness discipline" and "spiritual practice". My guess is that the reason for that choice of terminology is similar to the reason why the Alcoholics Anonymous twelve-step programme does not mention 'God' but the 'Higher Power'. The word 'God' has been so abused by religious people that it is a real barrier to some. It would be tragic if some people were prevented by a mere choice of words from entering the mystery. I can't imagine that Jesus would be concerned about terminology; it was he who said, "It is not those who say 'Lord, Lord,' who will enter the kingdom of heaven, but everyone who does the will of my Father in heaven" (Matthew 7:21).

− 4 −
Meditation

Mantra

I was at a meditation meeting recently and the speaker used the word "mantra" at one stage. One of the people there reacted very crossly and said it was something that Christians should have nothing to do with. The speaker was very patient and tried to explain, but I think it upset everyone there. I heard later that the man was telling people not to go to that prayer meeting anymore because it was spreading heresy. Can a Christian use a mantra or should it be avoided? I try to do a bit of meditation myself and the mantra seemed a good idea. What do you think?

The word *'mantra'* is a Sanskrit word, and for a start it is just that: a word. To say that Christians should have nothing to do with mantras is like saying that Christians should have nothing to do with words. The use of mantras (though not under that name of course) goes back to the early centuries of the Church. Mantras have a practical use: our concentration is mostly flickering and intermittent, and the repetition of a sacred word is an aid to concentration in prayer.

Here is what the author of the fourteenth-century Christian classic, *The Cloud of Unknowing*, wrote about it: "Take a short word, preferably of one syllable…. The shorter the word the better, being more like the working of the Spirit. A word like 'God' or 'Love'. Chose which you like, or perhaps some other, so long as it is of one syllable. And fix this word fast to your heart, so that it is always there come what may. It will be your shield and spear in peace and war alike. With this word you will hammer the cloud and the darkness above you. With this word you will suppress all thought…."

When Christians speak about 'mantra' they are using the Sanskrit word to refer to something that is part of the Christian tradition – because the Christian tradition did not supply a word for it. Let's not be scared off by a word. English is brim full of words from every part of the world. *Bungalow*, for example, is a Hindi word; (also, for good measure, a great many things we would regard as very domestically our own: *bangle, cot, dungarees, shampoo,* etc. etc.)

But one word in particular ought to be of special interest to witch-hunters: the word *'juggernaut'*. It should strike terror into them, because it is named after Juganath, a Hindu god whose image is carried in procession around the towns once a year in a huge cart. No, we mustn't react to words in a silly frightened way. That person's reaction to 'mantra' is not due to deeper insight or greater fidelity to the faith, but to ignorance.

If you want to follow up on contemplative prayer using a mantra, look at the website of the World Community for Christian Meditation (just google wccm). There you will find useful information, profound teaching, and a list of local contacts. It is a method of contemplative prayer, based on the Christian tradition and adapted for modern use, devised by John Main, a Benedictine monk (1926-1982). The movement is now worldwide. Click on your part of the map of the world and you will see local information. You can also have a weekly teaching posted to your email address.

Distraction

I took up meditation about three months ago and I think it's helping me. I do it every morning as soon as I get up. But the very minute I sit down I find distractions pouring in. I start thinking about my husband and my children and their problems, about the future, about the washing and the wash-up. What can I do to stop these distractions? I used to find it very peaceful, but now I don't know. Is there something wrong with me? Please tell me something that would help me.

We are all like you! That's the way the mind is. What I offer you is not really an answer but some kind of encouragement to keep going. At the heart of your own question you will find the answer that is right for you. A question is like a door opening, an answer is sometimes like a door closing.

The fact that you want to meditate, and that you do so every day, is the clearest possible commitment; it's a kind of love. You want to be there, even when you don't feel that you are getting anything out of it. That fidelity is something perfect. Every day you are there for your husband and children: that's already a way of being there for God. Now, in the last few months, you want to be there for God in this very explicit way. That wanting is the main thing. What goes on in your head after that is secondary. That's how it is in family, and I hope that's how it is with meditation. Meditation is like marriage: you take it on for better or worse, for richer or poorer, in sickness and in health, till death do us part. Ideas such as 'success', 'progress', 'perfection', are enemies of meditation (and perhaps enemies of marriage too). They are only ideas and judgments; don't put your meditation in such company. Put it with things like cooking, eating, brushing your teeth, putting out the rubbish…. It has to become a part of your ordinary day. It has to become nothing special. Special things are only for special times or special people or special places, but meditation is for always.

During meditation our defences are down: we are just there, a sitting target for whatever comes to us. The first thing we are aware of usually is how restless and noisy the mind is. There is a lot of 'static' when we are not tuned to the present moment – static and a confusion of sounds. But behind all that noise there is a background of silence. This silence is at the back of everything: it is the absolute background. We don't have to go searching for it; it is there all the time, but the noise is concealing it.

If only we could turn off that noise, that compulsive thinking! If only there were an off-button! Well, in a way, there is! Here is a piece of good advice: "Try a little experiment. Close your eyes and say to yourself: 'I wonder what my next thought is going to be.' Then become very alert and wait for the next thought. Be like a cat watching a mouse hole. What thought is going to come out of the mouse hole? Try it now." (Eckhart Tolle, *The Power of Now*). What we find is that we have to wait longer than we expected. During those moments when we were just alert and waiting, we were meditating. That's the off-button. Now we know! But let's not be disappointed when thoughts sneak in again (disappointment would show that we were working out of some idea of 'success'). We just become alert again – and again, and again…. That's the work of meditation.

Some thoughts are just vaguely hovering and they happen to get sucked into the mind, but other thoughts seem to have an energy of their own – sometimes very powerful – and they come straight at you. Thoughts that are shaped and driven by anger, or fear, or a habit of greed, tend to be very powerful and they try to force their way in (or is it that we powerfully attract them?). These have something to tell us, or rather show us. If we lose our sense of presence we are away over the hills with them, adding new thoughts to them, identifying ourselves with them, rationalising once again the fear or the anger or the greed…. But if we can just look at them without identifying ourselves with them, if we can let ourselves *experience the feeling without going into the story yet again*, if we can regard them just as traffic that is passing while we hold our station, then their visit will have been turned to good. We will have experienced that feeling directly, without self-defence, without projection, without a drama or a story; and that is what it needed most of all.

We won't feel that we have 'done' anything (meditation relieves us of the idea of 'achievement', as it relieves us of 'success', etc.). We may get up from our meditation, feeling that we have gained nothing (it relieves us of the idea of 'acquisition' too). But later on when we meet the person who triggered our anger or fear, etc., we just may see a difference, or the beginning of a difference. That is the fruit of meditation (as long as we don't look for it!).

'But where does God come into this?' one may ask. I would reply that God doesn't 'come into' anything, because God is already there. God is in everything, all Christian teachers have tried to tell us. We go searching for God as if God were lost. In the fifth century St Augustine put a shape on this searching for God. Let me quote you this famous paragraph from his *Confessions*:

> Late have I loved you, O Beauty, so ancient and so new, late have I loved you! And behold, you were within me and I was outside, and there I sought you, and in my deformity I fell upon those lovely things of your creation. You were with me but I was not with you. The beautiful things of this world kept me far from you, and yet if they had not been in you they would not have existed at all. You called me; you cried aloud to me; you broke through my barrier of deafness. You shone upon me; your radiance enveloped me; you put my blindness to flight. You shed your fragrance about me; I drew breath and now I gasp for you. I tasted you, and now I hunger and thirst for you. You touched me and I burned for your peace.

In this translation there are 146 words, but in the original Latin there are only 82 – and 26 of those are words of two letters or just one! It is a beautiful piece of writing (Latin was St Augustine's native language), and notice that it includes *all five senses*. The search for God is not a search for a formula or an answer or an explanation to satisfy the mind…. It is a search that involves us in our entire being: body, soul, and spirit, and every faculty. No one was more conscious than Augustine that it is a two-way search: the real search is *God's search for us*; we are the ones who are lost. Or rather we think and feel that we are lost, though we have the Christ-nature in us. We are just to lay our hearts open and uncluttered: then we may occasionally catch a hint of the One who is searching for us.

Why meditation?

I try to meditate with reasonable regularity, but I find it hard to stay at it, to stay motivated. Any tips?

My first would be regularity. Regularity is the key. If you do it regularly – I mean every day – it stops being a burden after a while; it becomes a natural part of your day, and you would no more want to drop it than you would want to drop breakfast or brushing your teeth.

Which is more natural, to meditate or not to meditate? Until I can say it's more natural to meditate than not to meditate, it will remain a burden, something I have to motivate myself to do. We give reasons for things that we consider optional. But what are your reasons for breathing? What are your reasons for sleeping? For eating? For doing anything that it normal and natural? We don't need to give ourselves reasons for doing these things. On the contrary, we would need to have very good reasons for not doing them. "To seek aright is easier and more natural to us than breathing," wrote the seventeenth-century French mystic, Jeanne-Marie Guyon.

If you commit yourself wholeheartedly to a practice of meditation, you will no longer need reasons for doing it; you will need reasons for not doing it. I find I have only a limited belief in reasons. Reasons can be shifty things; the mind is very clever and can just as readily find reasons for doing the opposite. When you hear a lot of reasons you sense some kind of reluctance. There is nothing wrong with the rational mind in itself, it is one of God's gifts to us; but it has a habit of taking itself to be the only source of wisdom. Then it tries to impose its edicts, and this makes you a divided kingdom: part of you wants to meditate and the parts that haven't been consulted don't. This is the root of all that resistance. The mediaevals thought of the human faculties as a kind of body politic, with reason as ruler. Very well, but if the fundamental image is ruling and politics, then what you get is politics all the way through. The faculty of will then becomes the big boss, and all the other faculties are under suspicion of being dissidents and subversives. No, keep politics outside the skin! (Think of reason, if you must, not as a separate 'faculty' but as the clarity of all the 'faculties'.)

In the past people used to marry for reasons, but the reasons had to evolve into something less political and controlling if the marriage was to be a true marriage; you couldn't spend a whole lifetime married for reasons. Likewise meditation. I often think of commitment to meditation as a sort of marriage. If you take it up, it has to be "for better, for worse; for richer, for poorer; in sickness and in health, until death do us part." Like marriage it has to penetrate the ego, and our rationality is so used to being in the service of the ego that we have to treat it with some suspicion and look for surer footing in a wider place.

I hope this doesn't dishearten you in any way. My intention is the opposite. When I say our commitment must be wholehearted I don't mean that we should meditate all day! I mean that if we meditate even for just five minutes, we should do it wholeheartedly. This makes it easier, in fact. A lot of energy is drained away by reluctance and indecision: dawdling is exhausting, as well as being a complete waste. Rather than waste your energy in that way put it into meditation. Then you may find that you are able to meditate for half an hour, or an hour, or even much more!

More natural to meditate than not to meditate? Yes, when you are doing nothing, do nothing. We have all the means of filling empty spaces today: TV, CDs, DVDs, computer games, a bewildering variety of magazines, piped music in supermarkets and churches.... It indicates how terrified we are of silence. It is not natural, it's a neurosis. It is more natural to meditate than not to meditate.

This thought also protects you from a very insidious temptation in religion: the feeling that you deserve brownie points for doing good. You have been a good boy, obeying the ruler reason, and you deserve a treat! But good is its own reason and its own reward. "If you ask a good person, 'Why are you doing good?'" said Meister Eckhart, "he [or she] will reply, 'For goodness' sake!' 'Why do you love God?' 'For God's sake!'"

My second tip: join a meditation group if possible. These usually meet only once a week, but that is a support structure for your daily meditation. You may have some searching to do before you find one that is right for you. Meditation is counter-cultural, so we need some support to stay with it. If you don't find one, you can still create a structure for yourself – by meditating always at the same time and in the same place.

How long?

I notice your comments on meditation from time to time. I do a bit of medi-tation myself a couple of times a week. I'm just wondering now how much of it I should do. Is there a minimum and a maximum? What would you recommend?

As I came downstairs many times a day (when I lived in Cork) I couldn't help noticing through a window an elderly couple in their house across the street. I noticed a vague question in my mind one day: Why are they always there? Then immediately I saw what a dumb question it was. They are there because they are at home. They don't need a reason to be there; they would need a reason to be somewhere else, but they need no reason to be at home. Home is where you don't need a reason to be. It helped me with meditation. Meditation is home. Meditation is when you are not away from your own reality. In computer language, it's meant to be our default mode. We need a reason for doing most things, but we don't need a reason to meditate. Thich Nhat Hanh tells people to say (silently) at every moment, "I have arrived, I have arrived, I am home!"

We sometimes find it hard to meditate, just as we are sometimes rest-less at home and looking for distractions such as TV. My home is only a house, not a real home, if I am unable to be quite unoccupied there when there is nothing that needs to be done. Meditation is the home of home. If I know that home and can return there anytime, I can be deeply at home no matter where I am.

Is there a recommended length of time for meditation? Is there a maximum and a minimum? The ideal is that I would be fully present and at home at every moment of the day: that's the maximum! The minimum is one instant! In practice we need to devote a certain amount of time consciously to just sitting in meditation every day. I could say to myself: I'll just try to be aware in everything I do, so there's no need to set aside a special time. But my every-minute awareness would be very wispy and shallow; and I would not be aware of that fact, because I would have nothing to compare it with. So it is necessary to set aside a special time, and then try to bring that awareness into the rest of the day. How much time? I won't say, because I'm not you. To attempt too much too soon might give you a surfeit. Begin with a short time: ten or fifteen minutes. Then as time goes by, you may increase it. You will know from the inside what is the right length of time; meditation itself will teach you.

It is very helpful to meditate with a group on a regular basis, if that is possible for you. Of course you are not limited to the amount of time the group spends in meditation. Somewhere between the minimum and the maximum is the optimum – that's the one to look for!

Silence of the heart

I've spent half an hour meditating every morning for the last month (except Sunday mornings).... I follow the method of concentrating on the breath. But I find that my mind is very busy and it takes ages to get right down to being quiet. I know the answer – concentrate on the breath! But is there some method for doing that more effectively...?

A method of putting the method into effect: that could go on to infinity! Just concentrate on the breath. Concentrate on it as if you had never drawn breath before – as if no one in the world had ever done so. It is hard to see something in all its particularity, because we are drunk on language. All language is abstract, except sounds like *ouch!* and *ugh!* – if they are language. The word 'tree', for example, is supposed to be a concrete noun, according to the grammar books. But can you see how *abstract* it is? Compared to the tree at my window, it is an abstraction. Likewise the breath: draw your breath as *this* breath, not breath in general, or one of a thousand breaths. The breath you drew a moment ago is of no use to you now, just as the breath you will draw in the future is of no use now. The only breath that works for you is the breath you are drawing *now*. Breathing is always in the present. It is like an anchor in the present moment. Hold you attention on your breath and you are guaranteed to be living in the Now.

See if this helps. There are times when the mind is like a stream rushing purposefully on its course. But often it is just meandering, and sometimes almost stopped. When you are sitting in meditation, facing a wall or whatever, in theory the mind should be stopped. Instead, it seems to keep on moving pointlessly. You see the movement in the dead leaves and twigs floating on the surface – images, memories, scraps of language…. What keeps them still moving? In a word, I think *desire* keeps them moving. The heart is as addicted to desiring as the mind is to meandering. Even after we have chosen to be where we are, we keep vaguely wishing we were elsewhere, or different, or doing something else, or with someone else…. We keep picturing what *could* be, rather than sinking into what is.

Or, depending on temperament, we think of what *should* be. That is also a kind of desire. This is the force that keeps the rubbish moving around. The moment you become aware of it, you neutralise it. Or I should say: your very awareness of it neutralises it. When it is not active you have what you might call silence of the heart. There is no silence of the mind if there isn't silence of the heart.

But don't carry this imagery into meditation with you. Forget about stagnant pools, etc. Imagery is a little less abstract than abstract description, but don't make a business of it. It is just a way of speaking. When you are sitting in meditation, concentrate on your breath, always this breath, and don't give up!

The Holy of Holies

You must be tired of people asking you about meditation. I hope you don't mind another question on the subject. I joined a meditation group a few months ago. We meet once a week, and I try to meditate every day at home but I don't feel I'm really in it. I feel nothing, I just go through it and nothing happens, I don't think I'm in contact with God at all. Sometimes I'm daydreaming and sometimes I'm just a blank. I don't feel that I am meditating at all. I'm ashamed to admit to the others how poor my performance is. Am I doing something wrong? What should it be like if I was doing it right? I would be glad to hear your thoughts on the subject.

There is really no such thing as meditation; there are just people who meditate. The question is not separate from the person asking it. You don't need to be ashamed of your performance, because meditation is not a performance; and besides, everyone in your group is struggling just like you.

Most people come to meditation with some expectations: they want it to be some kind of experience that they have read or heard about, or they want it to produce certain results. All such expectations are a hindrance, because they are about the past or the future, not about the present.

The word 'present' is the key to it; or the word 'now'. Everyone I've met in the last couple of years seems to have read, or to be reading, Eckhart Tolle's *Power of Now*. 'Now' is a short word, and what it refers to is even shorter: the present moment has no duration at all. There's no time in it for thoughts or expectations.

When you take these out, what's left? When you take out all the furniture a room looks very bare! Two lines from W.B. Yeats: "At stroke of midnight soul cannot endure / A bodily or mental furniture." Meditation is that fleeting instant between past and future, just as midnight is the invisible frontier between one day and the next. There's no time for the mind to latch on to a thought, or for the feelings to unroll themselves – because the next moment has already arrived. Meditation is totally simple, and for that very reason it is difficult! Why, because we are much more used to dealing with mental content than with inner space itself. We make a *room* in our house – a word that means 'space' – and we immediately fill it with furniture, making it less and less a room! Many people can't endure an empty space on a wall; they have to hang something there. It's like baroque art and architecture: all decoration, no background.

When you sit in an empty room you are more aware of the absence of decoration than of the room itself. There's a lot to think and say and feel about decoration, but nothing to say about the empty space. You can't put it 'out there' or 'in front of' your mind to think about it, because you are in it; it encloses you; it is nearer to you than all decoration. The mind is like that. You are it. It is something you look out from, rather than something you can look at.

So if you feel that you are nothing when you meditate, that's good! It means that you have become free for a moment of all mental furniture and decoration, and you are in touch with your true nature: which is, as Johann Tauler put it, "an empty place where God may do God's work." Your own "emptiness", as the saints have called it, is the place of meeting with God – who is not another piece of decoration.

The Holy of Holies – the innermost space in the Temple in Jerusalem, where only the high priest could enter once a year – was completely empty in the time of Jesus. It was "the place of meeting" with God. All our words and images, which are so useful and necessary, are left at the entrance to the Holy of Holies.

At the moment of Jesus' death, the gospels say, "the veil of the Temple was torn in two from top to bottom" (Matthew 27:51; Mark 15:38; Luke 23:45). This was the veil in front of the Holy of Holies. What was the meaning of this? That moment was the spiritual equivalent of the Big Bang that astrophysicists speak of. St Paul interpreted it to mean that *we* are now the Holy of Holies. "Do you not know that you are God's temple?" (1 Corinthians 3:16). It seems we have to get used to being an empty space, a temple for God.

Just as our own nature is deeper than all the thoughts and images that pass through our minds (even thoughts and images of ourselves), God's nature too is beyond all our thoughts and images. To identify God with our thoughts and images of God would clearly be idolatry. The word 'idolatry' is from a combination of two Greek words, *eidōlon* (image) and *latreia* (adoration). Idolatry is the worship of images. In meditation we are becoming free of that trap.

How can we persuade ourselves to enter our Holy of Holies and stay there for some time without bringing our stuff with us? The John Main tradition (and others too) suggests the use of a mantra, and in particular the word *Maranatha*. As you know, their answer to every difficulty in meditation is: return to the repetition of the mantra. This cuts through all the entanglements of thoughts and images. It is very effective. Others suggest just following the breath, which has the same effect – the breath being like a mantra without words. They all advise us not to become discouraged when our minds wander and we begin to daydream. Just quietly return to the mantra, or to following the breath. If you feel nothing, that's far from being a problem. If you think nothing is happening, don't worry. Just keep going, and don't be watching your performance. Just keep doing it, knowing that your sheer presence by itself is your contact with God. If you really are in the Holy of Holies, there's nothing and no one to meet except God, who is beyond thought and images. "Do you not know that you are God's temple and that God's Spirit dwells in you?"

"Am I doing something wrong?" you asked. From reading your letter, my guess is that you are doing it right. The only thing that seems wrong is your habit of checking and assessing your performance. When you do that you are not allowing the mantra (or the breath) to turn in you, like a wheel. You are putting a stick in the spokes.

Meditation – or the real world?

I notice that you write about meditation a lot. Not meaning to be offensive, could you write about something else for a change? Meditation seems to be a very subjective thing and when there are so many real problems in the Church like child abuse why don't you write about them? What we need now is to deal with real problems.... There's a real world out there and we need to be objective.

By asking this question you are forcing me to write once more about meditation! In fact I just try to give replies to the questions I'm asked.

Someone asked me the other day how people who have had spiritual experiences get back to ordinary reality afterwards. I replied that they have no trouble, because they haven't been anywhere. Meditation is not about going into an alternative reality (can there be such a thing?); it is about going more deeply into this one.

I always shift in my seat when someone talks about 'the real world out there'. There is only one world, and it includes us human beings with all our thoughts and hopes and fantasies; it includes our 'subjectivity', if we have to use that word. We shouldn't imagine the subjective and the objective as alternative worlds that we can choose between. There is ultimately no way to avoid facing what we call our subjectivity. We don't become 'objective' by ignoring or denying subjectivity. If we haven't faced our own subjectivity we don't know what we are doing in the 'objective' world. Modern history is rich in examples of dictators who brutally imposed their own unexamined egos on whole populations.

Undesirable as it might appear to many people, the question of subjectivity keeps on arising. Modern popular culture is seriously messed up at this level. We love to read about people in the papers (and if that isn't turning them into objects, what is?), but what we want to get at is their subjectivity. We want to get inside the minds of public figures – politicians, actors and celebrities. We want to know 'objectively' what these people feel subjectively. It's a form of pornography: it is an attempt to access subjectivity 'objectively'. You may remember T.S. Eliot's indictment of the twentieth century: it will be remembered, he said, as a time when people "fornicated and read the papers."

I am convinced of the practical necessity of meditation. It is a determined effort to confront our own subjectivity in the interests of our real life and the lives of the people we live with – in the interests of 'the real world out there', as you call it. What would Mahatma Ghandi have been if he had never meditated? What would Hitler have been if he had?

Meditation doesn't impose itself as an urgent necessity. In the world of advertising, in which we are steeped, the real urgent necessities are fashion accessories, convenience foods, and electronic gadgets. I've no doubt you will agree that no one can live on these alone. But even if we manage to ignore the products on offer we are still in danger of being controlled by the mind that underlies them: a mind that says the remedy for our ills lies in yet another product 'out there'. The so-called 'real world' is mind-made. Meditation is about having a different mind, "a new mind," St Paul called it. It doesn't impose itself as an urgent necessity, but it is probably the most urgent of all.

I hope the meaning of meditation will click for you sometime, Joe. In the meantime don't be put off by anything I say about it. It is more than all of us. It is simpler than any of us. It reveals itself to us when we are pulled out from under the mind-made world and become simple like children. It is the depth that is "hidden from the wise and the intelligent and revealed to infants" (Luke 10:21).

Scattered mind

I want to get some help with my struggle with meditation. I've read a lot of books about it and they are all great until I sit down to do it. Then my mind takes off and all the things I read about are miles away. Even when I pick up the book I've been reading and read a paragraph that I marked, it doesn't make it happen for me. I'm better at reading about it than doing it. I often say if there was someone inside my head to direct the traffic I'd be OK. I know you can't do that, but you may be able to give me a few tips.

That's an interesting thought: an inner traffic cop who would tell you where to park and where not to park. Some people would tell you that you have to be that traffic cop yourself, but I'd rather say you should give up the idea of directing that inner traffic. Thoughts move: it is their nature to move; when they stop they don't exist. When you get involved with them – *whether to follow them or to stop them* – you are keeping them in existence. Instead, just *watch* them without judging them or telling them where to go or trying to stop them. Watch from the side, as if they had nothing to do with you. In a real sense they don't: they are just the world's debris blowing through you.

People sometimes say "I'm 'into' this or that." They mean they have an interest in it. An interest in meditation isn't enough; you have to be into it in a full sense. Nothing will take you anywhere unless you are inside it. To the extent that you are trying to direct your mental traffic you are not yet inside meditation.

When are you 'inside' meditation? I suggested above that you should "watch from the side". That watching from the side is meditation. Which side is it? Left? Right? No, it is *every* side: it's the whole background to all traffic. If it were one particular side you would be scrambling to get there. But you are there already: that whole background is your true nature.

How we would all love to grab it and hold onto it! My true nature: a prize catch. But the very effort to do so would turn it into an object – in other words, another item of traffic. If it could be caught it would be another foreground object – a big one, but still just an object. There is nothing that can be caught, so give up all attempts to catch it. The real background, your true nature, is yours already before you thought of trying to catch it. It was yours even before you developed an interest in meditation.

That leaves you with nothing to do. But people speak of 'doing their meditation', don't they? Yes, but that is an external description, like entering an item on a timetable. It's true that we have to put it on a timetable; we have to have a daily routine of meditation. But when you sit down to meditate you are not doing anything; you are just watching. At that point the traffic will try to pull you again into its stream. It will urge you to pick up a book, or to check how you are doing, or even to check the time…. But relax, don't do anything.

That sounds really easy, but as you know it is not easy. There are two kinds of laziness: one is a reluctance to do anything, the other is a reluctance to do nothing. Doing nothing is harder for us today: we live in a fog of activism, a fog so dense that we can't easily see through it or around it. We are over-stimulated and to that extent we are unwell. We need to recover, to convalesce. If you have ever had to convalesce after an illness, you have a useful marker. The doctor – and everyone else – will tell you, "You just need to rest." Meditation is like that: just rest, don't be restless to get going.

You will notice that there is nothing here for the ego: no sense of achievement, no sense of making progress, no sense of acquiring something you set out to acquire. If you feel the pinch of that, it is a good sign:

you could be on the right track.

Messy meditation

I'm doing my best with meditation but it's defeating me, I have to admit now after four or five years of it. My mind has a life of its own and I can't stay still for five minutes, let alone 20 or 30. I've read the answers you gave to other people who asked about meditation but I think I'm a worse case than any of them. Is there anything very simple and basic you could tell me that might help?

If you are doing your best, as you say, then you couldn't possibly do better than that at present!

You may be saying to yourself now as you read this: "Oh I didn't mean I'm doing my *absolute* best; I only mean that I'm hanging on somehow." But I want to say: The accusing thought of the absolute best could still be lurking there in the shadows. Forget about your absolute best; none of us knows what our absolute best might be. In fact, the word 'absolute' would be a good one to drop completely. Have you noticed how overused it is now? It is beginning to replace the word 'yes'. "Did you feed the cat?" "Absolutely."

If it was only about the word it wouldn't be a big problem. But I think most people have expectations of themselves that are … absolute. By that I mean that most people have little or no patience with themselves or with their present state. We always want to be in a better state. When I said to a Zen master once in dokusan, "I'm making no progress," he replied instantly, *"There is no progress. There's nowhere to go. There's no distance."* And with that he struck his gong, which meant, "Go!" Go back and sit in your mess for another nine hours! Then we'll see, next time, if something has penetrated your skull!

We will never get anywhere unless we start from where we are. Dive into the mess and don't even think of wishing for a better place to be. Reality isn't somewhere else; it is right where you are. The only thing that is hiding it from you is your restlessness to be somewhere else. All our lives – especially in religion – we have been fed on a diet of idealism. That is why we stay exactly as we are throughout our whole adult lives. We cannot move on until we have made peace with the present. And the way to make peace with the present is to forget about moving on. It's paradoxical, I know, but that's the way it is.

In Christian terms we could say we die into the present moment and God raises us to new and deeper life. "Keep back nothing," wrote C.S. Lewis. "Nothing in you that has not died will ever be raised from the dead." The seed has to fall into the ground and die if there is to be new life. This new life is not a project but God's gift. You don't have to give yourself grades; you only have to hold your station. Sit as if you were going to spend the rest of your life sitting in this place. Of course the demands of practical life make that impossible in practice. But sit with the *mind* of someone who is going to stay here forever. That's not impossible.

We are all doing our best – not our absolute best, whatever that might mean, but the best we can do at the moment. Even a practising alcoholic is somehow doing the best that he or she can do *at this moment*. Resist the urge to give yourself a grade, because in the next moment it will be a degrade. Accept where you are; put down your roots there. That's where reality is; that is the only place where life can flow through you.

I find that if you have to talk to yourself about it, it is better to talk in images. To settle yourself at the beginning of your meditation, imagine, for example, a tree. Such stability, such strength! Its roots go down into the earth, further than we can ever follow. Such frightening shapes these have; but the tree draws its life and strength from them. And, above ground, what weather a tree endures! But through all the seasons it holds its station. In winter it loses all its leaves, in spring it gains new ones. It doesn't take fright and try to run away; it doesn't long to be in a better place. Trees are our oldest neighbours, and they have much to teach us, especially about meditation. The tree knows what the rest of us need to learn: there is nowhere to go, because we are already there; there is no distance.

Meditation adds up to a kind of love: not sentimental or self-indulgent or even self-conscious, but strong and silent and with the humility of the earth. St Paul wrote about being "rooted and grounded in love" (Ephesians 3:17). You are already that, Roy. May you blossom in every possible way!

Meister Eckhart

I was at a lecture by ... [a philosophy teacher] a few months ago, and he insisted that Meister Eckhart was a pantheist. When I found your website I searched for Meister Eckhart in it (knowing the Dominican connection) and I was surprised to see that you often quote him – and always approvingly. Was he knowingly a pantheist or is this the most recent understanding of his theories? Can a Christian be a pantheist in any sense of the word? I'd like to hear your views on this.

I deleted the name of your lecturer so that he could not be googled under this heading. I don't want to help ruin his career.

No, Meister Eckhart was not a pantheist, though it's easy enough to understand how someone might get that impression.

Pantheism is a philosophical view, a theory; but Meister Eckhart, though he had been an academic theologian, was speaking not from theory but from religious experience. These two perspectives are quite different from each other, and it is very interesting to look at this. Most of the confusion about mysticism is due to a failure to see this difference.

With very few exceptions the philosophical view is a view from the outside. Philosophers join hands with journalists in what Jonathan Swift called "the tribes of Answerers, Considerers, Observers, Reflectors, Detectors, Remarkers." A German philosopher, Ernst Jünger, called this kind of seeing "an act of aggression". The great sponsor of this kind of seeing was an earlier German philosopher, Immanuel Kant, who elaborated a view that made contemplation impossible in principle. The mediaevals had distinguished between the active and passive functions of the mind; they called them *ratio* and *intellectus*. *Ratio* is the discursive mind, while *intellectus* is the intuitive. But Kant dismissed *intellectus* as mere confusion and lent all his weight to *ratio*. The mind's proper activities, he said, were analysing, distinguishing, comparing, relating, abstracting, deducing, demonstrating.... These were "work", he said; it was *serious* work, he said, while the contemplative view was self-indulgent. He was the common ancestor of Swift's tribes. Many a philosopher (or even a philosophy teacher) surveys a subject in the way a butcher surveys a carcass. I know that mind, because I was a philosophy teacher myself for a number of years.

When Meister Eckhart said that at the deepest level of spiritual life, "whoever sees God sees nothing but one," or when his follower Johann Tauler said the soul "knows nothing of difference from God," they were not giving expression to a *theory* they had arrived at by thinking – just as when Julian of Norwich wrote, "I saw no difference between God and our substance, but, as it were, all God," she was not giving us a conclusion she had reached through study and reflection. It is easy to understand how such expressions scandalise people who are unaware of the distinction between *ratio* and *intellectus*.

Julian was more careful than Eckhart in explaining herself. Having just said that she saw "no difference between God and our substance," she immediately added: "and still my understanding accepted that our substance is in God, that is to say that God is God, and our substance is a creature in God." Her first expression is from *intellectus*, the second from *ratio*. This is how the two functions work together, as the mediaevals understood.

Eckhart too can be careful when he wants to. He repeatedly says (like Julian) that "the creature is *in* God," and "God is *in* every creature." This is no more or less than what the great multitude of Christian writers have said throughout the centuries. Someone coined a word for it: panentheism. Pantheism would be the belief that everything is God; this could never be an orthodox Christian view. But panentheism is the belief that everything is *in* God; this view is perfectly orthodox.

It is interesting to see Eckhart's younger contemporaries defending and explaining him. Johann Tauler said to a group: "There was one great teacher who taught you and told you about these things; but you did not understand him." And Henry Suso refers to "the sweet teachings of holy Meister Eckhart," and said to someone, in reference to Eckhart's teaching: "Your problem is without doubt that you do not understand the distinction previously mentioned about how a person should become one [with God] in Christ and yet remain distinct, and how he is united, but perceives himself to be one and not just united."

These people were trying to put words on their experience, much as St Paul tried to put words on his experience on the road to Damascus. During the time when we are completely absorbed in something – even a sunset or a piece of music – we perceive no distinction between it and ourselves. It is the same with moments of absorption in God. Then, in Tauler's words (quoted above in part), the soul "loses itself, and knows nothing of God or of itself, of likeness to God or of difference from God, or of anything whatsoever." Then we return to ordinary consciousness and become well aware of the difference.

I hope these thoughts will help to clarify the confusion sown by your philosophy teacher. And I hope the effect of his teaching is not to inoculate you against thinking. Good luck.

Living in the now

It was the same again this summer. I was at a retreat and the retreat director went on and on about living in the now. I have to say I'm tired of hearing about the now. It's only in the past few years. Before that we never heard about the now. What's wrong? Are people ashamed of the past or what? Every book on spirituality you pick up now is about the now. Shouldn't there be some kind of balance? Our past made us what we are and we shouldn't be ashamed of it. I'm asking you because you write a lot about it too. I'm sure it suits a lot of people to write about the now when they don't know much about the past.... Any comment?

Every moment of our life is new and original; it is not a repetition of a previous moment. It is like a snowflake: it has a unique pattern and it vanishes immediately. In a strict sense, nothing exists except what exists now. That does not mean that the past never happened, or that what happened in the past has no interest for us now. To stress the unique reality of now is not to dismiss the past.

I spend a lot of my time reading the early and mediaeval Christian writers, as well as many others from later centuries. Some of what they wrote, centuries ago, is of great interest and significance to us still. When their writing seems at times vague to us and far from experience, it says nothing to us now; but it may have said a little or a lot to their contemporaries. When it was written from real experience it tends to last forever, leaping over the centuries. At their best those writers wrote in the now – *their* now. When we read what they wrote we are reading in *our* now. When there is a match, the text jumps off the page. If this is the case with the classics of spirituality, how much more when we read the Scriptures – especially in the Liturgy?

Nothing and no one ever exists except in the now. This is common-place understanding today, but of course when something is mentioned repeatedly we get tired of listening. When we talk a lot, there is a risk that talking will become a substitute for the real thing. However, it is still important to remind ourselves and one another to live in the reality of the present moment rather than in memories of the past. But if we only *talk* about it we soon sicken of the words; we have to *do* something about it. "Be doers of the word, and not merely hearers who deceive themselves" (James 1:22). One very useful thing we can do is meditation. As soon as we begin a practice of meditation we get moment by moment reminders of how hard it is to sit still and live in the present for longer than a couple of seconds at a time. Pascal famously said, "All human evil comes from a single cause, human beings' inability to sit still in a room." We have to persevere with our practice, seeing ever more clearly how scattered our minds are, how accustomed we have become to living in fantasy and confusion.

The present moment appears very brief and (when we sit still) very empty. This is why we look for something larger and more exciting. But this is an attempt to escape from our own reality. Living in the present moment is often less exciting than memory or fantasy, and being faithful to it is a hard discipline. Someone asked me once if meditation was a flight from reality. On the contrary it is like a sharp drill for boring down into it. Reality isn't guaranteed. What we describe as reality is often a mix of day-dreaming, thinking, planning, imagining, hating, longing....

Once as I watched a troubled young couple being married I began to estimate the number of people standing before the altar: there was the visible couple standing there (that's two); then there was his idea of who he was, and her idea of who she was (that makes four); then his idea of her, and her idea of him (that's six). I didn't know them very well, but I supposed that he had an idea of who she *should be*, as she had an idea of what he *should be.* That would bring it up to eight.... All but two of those people will have to die away, leaving just the real couple. It has to be so if the marriage is to last. It is a challenging adventure. Whether married or not, we all have a lot of dying to do. We are married to reality, but that is often a dysfunctional marriage. Trying to live in the now is not an easy option; it is not an escape from anything, just as marriage is not an escape; it is a determined effort to die to our false self, "to wither into the truth," as Yeats put it.

I hope the retreat director had you meditating on that retreat. If not, then he or she was in danger of substituting words for reality. A priest had preached enthusiastically about marriage. As the congregation left the church one woman said to another: "I wish I knew as little about marriage as that young man!" You have realised, Eleanor, that words by themselves are not enough. That is a major step. Don't give up!

− 5 −
The Ego

What is the ego?

I notice you often talk about ego and always negatively. Is it such a bad thing? If it is such a bad thing why didn't we hear more about it in the past? I'd prefer it any day to the collective mentality, to everyone letting on to be different while really being the same, going to the same places for holidays and wearing the same clothes and watching the same TV programmes. There are very few individuals around…. What the world needs is more ego, not less…. I'd like to hear what you have to say about it when someone like me casts doubt on it.

To begin at the beginning: *ego* is the Latin (and Greek) pronoun for 'I'. There's nothing wrong with any pronoun in itself. The ambiguity lies in its reference. When I say 'I', am I referring to my real identity or just to my self-image? Jesus often referred to himself ("I am the bread of life … I am the good shepherd … I am the way, the truth and the life…."), but it is impossible to imagine him just presenting a 'face' to the public. The trouble is that our own masks cling so close to us that we are normally unaware of them as masks, and so we take them for reality. "This is who I really am," we say, but it is usually just a narrow selection of self-images and memories that I have allowed to define me. My ego is not the identity God creates in me, but the one I create for myself (in collusion with other people). This contraction of my true identity can't be a good thing.

The Christian faith is seldom allowed to challenge the ego; instead it has been used to extend it to infinity. There has been a great naivety about the ego in most Christian writing, even though the New Testament is clear about "dying to oneself". We take up John of the Cross and read about "the dark night of the soul," but we tend to see this as something so extreme that it is only for "chosen souls" (that ugly phrase), and not for every Christian. Certainly we heard about "self-denial," but this was just a practice of foregoing pleasures. No one seemed to notice that it is a perfect double-bind, raising a crucial question about identity. We are more likely today to ask that question, "*Who* is this self that is attempting to deny itself?" And we have been given a name for it: there is a great likelihood that it is the ego.

I remember a children's game where you had to have rapid dialogue with someone while avoiding the words 'yes', 'I' and 'no'. But trying to be free of ego is much more difficult than avoiding the word 'I'. Mind you, it might not be a bad place to start! A Taiwanese confrère came to our community to learn English. He was a beginner, so it was a long and difficult struggle for him. I was waiting for the day when he knew enough English to be able to tell me what his impression of English was: what were the strangest things about it. It is hard if not impossible for us to see our own language from the outside, but he was more an outsider to it than anyone I had met. After about six months I was able to ask. With great diffidence and politeness he eventually said, "English is all 'I'. Every sentence, 'I'. And you write it with a capital letter – like God!" It was one of the best lessons I had ever had – well worth waiting six months for. After that, I began to pay attention to the way he said things, not judging it now as just faulty grammar. One morning at the beginning of summer I met him on the stairs and he said, "Today, for the first time, short sleeves!" And did you notice? – no 'I'. In very many situations the 'I' isn't necessary; it is something added.

The ego is a subtle enemy, partly because it is not an enemy on every occasion, and partly because our very struggle against it only strengthens it. Yes we do need egos; we need them as we need names: for handy reference and for general convenience. But when we were born we had neither names nor egos. The real self is part of the whole world, but the ego is an attempt to create a separate self. Construction begins early: when a child enters the No phase. Through saying No, the ego gains strength. As we grow up we learn that we have to modify this, or conceal its uglier aspects, but the basic structure remains intact. It is very difficult to dismantle.

Try this image. Think of how a jackdaw builds its nest in a chimney. It keeps dropping in sticks till one of them lodges itself by chance across the empty space. The next stick lodges more easily, and soon every stick lodges there as they build up to a secure platform. Any downward pressure will make it even more secure. It seems quite solid, but it is sitting on emptiness – an emptiness that the jackdaw no longer notices. We are sitting on emptiness, an emptiness that we rarely glimpse or want to glimpse. We maintain our nest, our ego, because we have invested everything in it. We keep adding to it all our life. If we hear great things about 'enlightenment' we may want to add that too. Such effort only wedges the ego more tightly, making it more and more secure.

You asked why we didn't hear more about the ego in the past. We heard a great deal about it, but not under the name 'ego'. There were images and stories from the gospels, for example about the seed falling into the ground and dying, because otherwise it would remain alone. So real were these sayings that Jesus himself was a perfect example of them. In the history of Christian spirituality there has been an extensive vocabulary of words like 'self-denial', 'self-abnegation', 'detachment', even 'emptiness', and 'nothing'. Many of them would send a chill through your spine. But it doesn't matter greatly which terms we use, so long as we keep our eyes open and our minds clear.

You contrasted ego with "the collective mentality, with everyone letting on to be different while really being the same." You put it very well. I remember an ad for car accessories: "Does your car look like a thousand others?" it asked. Of *course* it does! Quality control sees to that. So you know they are talking to you. Then they roll out their offer: "Get some of our accessories!" – which of course they produce by the thousand. So really your car will *still* look like a thousand others. And they would make it a million if they could. These little bursts of 'creativity' are all mass-produced, just like the cars. The ego too is always pretending to be different while being profoundly the same. It is not in contrast with the collective mentality; it *feeds* the collective mentality. Since it is based on nothing real it models itself by imitating others. It doesn't represent individuality at all. A real individual would live from his or her true nature and wouldn't worry about being different – *nor about being the same!*

Hate your ego?

I've been trying to work out what the ego is. You often write about it, and I've looked up all your past references to it. I ought to hate it by now I suppose, but I still have questions about it. "My ego is not the identity God creates in me, but the one I create for myself (in collusion with other people)," you wrote. And "The real self is part of the whole world, but the ego is an attempt to create a separate self." What is this separate self and where is it in me?

I hope I never said that you should hate your ego. There's not much to be gained by hating anything; that only ties us up with it in complicated ways. We have to *understand* our ego; or rather, we have to try and *see it at work*. We try to see it at work in order to be aware that we don't need to be controlled blindly by it at all times.

Many things that are simple in themselves become complicated the moment we begin to speak about them. Language is odd at times. We say things like, "It is raining." If someone were to ask, "*What* is raining?" we would think that that was an odd question, but the odd thing is the mention of an 'it' in the first place. I once remarked to an Italian that their language was free of that particular bit of nonsense (in Italian you just say '*piove*', with no 'it'). But he replied, "What we are really saying is '*esso piove*'." But that is something that Italians never say in fact! He had introduced an 'it' (*esso*) artificially – such is the addiction to turning everything into a 'thing', even in a language that doesn't encourage you to do so. Is rain a thing? If you say yes, you are thinking of rainwater, not of rain. Rain is rain only while it is falling. It is a *process*, not a thing.

This is all very trivial when it is only about the weather, and such ...

um! ... things. But when people start talking, for instance, about their marriage as if it were somehow 'out there', or about their life, the way is open for a lot of confused thinking. If you were to say that there is no such thing as marriage, people would accuse you of being against marriage; they would call you a libertine. But what is your marriage apart from the pair of you? Sometimes people ask what prayer is, or meditation. When asked such questions I tend to reply that there is no such thing as prayer, no such thing as meditation. There is just what you do and what God does. Likewise there is no such 'thing' as your ego; the word stands for a way of thinking about yourself and everything in you and around you.

If you were asked, "Who are you?" you would reply with your name. If you were asked, "What are you?" you would answer, "I'm a nurse, or a waiter, or a train-driver...." We take our *job* as our identity. All this is perfectly practical and normal – so long as nobody tries to *imprison* you in your name or your job. You would cringe, I think, if someone said, "Ah, so you're one of those Murphys!" or "So, you're just a waiter!" There's nothing wrong with being a Murphy, or with being a waiter, or even a waiter called Murphy. You don't have to hate yourself for it. But you know that while you are that, you are also more than that. Likewise there is nothing wrong with having (or rather, being) an ego; but you know that you are more than that.

Your ego is just a more extended sort of 'name' and 'job'. Like these, it is a superficial identity that links you into society. There is no need to think of it as some sort of mysterious *inner* kernel of your being. It is not your real self; it is all 'out there'. It is your whole personality (but not in a philosophical or theological sense). It is what you do and how you 'fit in' in every situation. The trouble is that we internalise it and make it our only identity. When it is really internalised, it is also how you feel. Sartre described a soldier in civilian dress walking down the street, or rather marching – because he had become a soldier to his very core; he had internalised his outer identity. Sartre called this "bad faith" (not in a religious sense, obviously).

The ego is not really an inner identity; it is external: it is *between* you and others. But then it tries to become your inner identity. A man told me recently that he spends "quality time" with himself every few days. But what do we return to when we return to ourselves? My answer is that it is very often to the *internalised ego*, like the soldier's. Our personality has followed us home. This isn't "quality time"; it's just more of the same – only *isolated* – it is the 'separate self'. So we are alone and yet not alone. There is no satisfaction; just the built-in frustration of the ego. Then the question arises: do we have an identity that lies deeper than this frustration?

This is the question of the true self, the quest of all real religious seekers. The mystics are the people who have found their way to it and can therefore guide us towards it – though they can never make us see it. That seeing (like all seeing) is something that only we can do for ourselves. They tell us that when we glimpse our true nature we see that we are deeply one with God, and with other people, and with everything around us. We will know ourselves so close to other people that they will appear to us as ourselves in another form. Each moment will be a fulfilment in itself, rather than a mad rush to the next moment and the next. In other words we will know what it is to be alive.

Judging people

Maybe you can help me now with something that bothers me a little, or more than a little. I have a habit of making very unkind judgements about some people. Even when they do good things I'm right in there with my judgement – he's just a hypocrite, or she's just trying to look good. I hate myself for this and I just wish it wasn't part of me.... Can you suggest a way of getting clear of this?

Jesus said, "Do not judge," but we have some investment in judging one another. It goes on and on, even when we know it is not right. Nor is it useful to us on the practical level. So it's a real puzzle. This suggests that it has deeper roots, or at any rate that its roots go down elsewhere.

I'll go straight to what I think is the point: the ego is not capable of stopping itself from judging, because it *exists* by judging. Judging is its lifeline, its oxygen. Just as you cannot kill yourself by just deciding to stop breathing, the ego by itself cannot stop judging.

"Do not judge, so that you may not be judged. For with the judgment you make you will be judged, and the measure you give will be the measure you get" (Matthew 7:1-2). How are we to read this text? Could God be as mean as we are? Could God's way of judging be as partial as ours? I think it means: the measure you give is the measure you are *capable* of receiving. We not only limit the other person by our judgments: we limit ourselves correspondingly. It has nothing to do with the great heart of God; it is about our own ego and its inability to love.

What is this ego, anyway? The ego is my image of who I am, the bag of experiences that define "me". Starting at a very early age I made (and continue to make) this collection by selecting some things (and experiences and people…) that I identify with, and excluding others. This is what I mean by saying that judging is the ego's lifeline. I become so used to this identification that I see it as my identity. So then, it is not only to a police officer that I "show my identification"; I am doing it all the time to everyone! This identification is not rock solid; it is a house built on sand, because experience is constantly changing, and so is one's interpretation of experience.

Talking about the ego is not some modern psychological fad, as some writer claimed. The word 'ego' is just the Latin word for 'I'. Henry Suso (fourteenth century) distinguished five meanings of 'I' or 'self'. The fifth, he said, "belongs to a person exclusively as his or her own, and it is one's individual human self." This corresponds to what we now call ego. Then he added, "Now what is it that leads people astray and robs them of happiness? It is exclusively this last self."

How are we to stop this ego from judging, since it has no capacity to do so itself? By making good judgments in place of bad? By saying that everything and everybody is wonderful? That would be dishonest, as well as being exhausting. And besides, it usually doesn't work. If we were on a moving train, it wouldn't matter much whether we walked towards the front or towards the back. If we wanted to stop moving, we would have to step off the train.

Meditation means stepping off the train. It means abandoning, as far as we are able at that moment, all our identifications. It is not so heroic; our identifications are not our identity, and the more often we disown them the more clearly we see that. Gradually we lose interest in judging other people; it doesn't make sense any more. Even Jesus doesn't judge the world ("I came not to judge the world, but to save the world" Jn 12:47), so what grounds could we have for doing so?

Persons

You said something once about personality that gave the impression you didn't think it was important. It comes back to my mind now and then. Could you elaborate?

Yes, we glorify personality. We even call some special people 'personalities'. If you say that some event will be packed with personalities, people will be very disappointed if they find just a lot of ordinary people there. Mind you, this narrowing of the word 'person' isn't due entirely to magazines such as *Hello*. When I lived in Rome years ago I was asked one day to accompany a cardinal on a trip. I hopped into the back of the car, the most suitable place for an ordinary man, I thought. But the cardinal (who was English-speaking) reproved me. "The custom here," he said, "is that the Person sits in the rear." That was a more exclusive use of 'person' than you will find in any celebrity magazine. The irony is that we were just going for a walk in a nearby park – which had no separate areas for 'Persons'.

So if we were to continue to rely on the word 'person' the first move should be to democratise it. We should wrest it from the clutches of the eminent and restore it to every human being. The much older understanding of 'person' was actually as wide as the human race. In fact it was wider. Scholastic theologians included angelic and divine persons as well as human. A person, said one of them, is "a *suppositum* which can say 'I,' which exists apart, which is *sui juris*." (For *'suppositum'* you can read 'unit'.) What do you think of that? Is it worth fighting for? I hardly think so.

The divine persons certainly don't "exist apart". The traditional doctrine of the Trinity (which these same Scholastics, of course, would defend) says that the divine persons "are constituted by their relationships to one another." In other words, it is their relationships to one another that make them who they are. (This has the paradoxical effect of saying that the Absolute is absolutely relative!)

As for human persons, there is some sense too in which we are what we are because of our relationships with one another. We would all be at a great disadvantage if we never had a mother, for example! Woody Allen said he was born in New York "because I wanted to be near my mother." Our mothers were the first, but not the last, who made us what we are. It is fascinating to read about feral children who grew up with no human contact from an early age. They were seen to have little or no self-awareness, they were incapable of social behaviour and (if found after the age of about twelve) incapable of learning speech. It takes a community to produce a functioning human being. So much for "existing apart".

The Scholastic definition of 'person' was purely abstract and had no connection with what people mean today by person or personality. I would enjoy seeing the word used less frequently. Nothing real would be lost. If instead of 'person' you just say 'human' you are on safer ground: it includes everything you want to include in 'person', but it has the advantage of not dignifying what is bad – 'human' includes good and bad alike. Under the heading of 'human' we could then talk with clarity about ego and true nature. The word 'personal' frequently dignifies a lot of stuff that is just an expression of ego. To see such stuff for what it is, is to clear the ground for discovery of our true nature. The true nature is the Christ-nature in us, as in St Paul's statement: "It is no longer I who live, but it is Christ who lives in me" (Galatians 2:20).

Christian spirituality has not challenged the ego with sufficient clarity, and I think this is because the word 'person' has stood in the way. It would be no loss to stop saying "I" all the time, and imagining that we "exist apart", and it would be no loss to our real dignity if we were to stop looking for special seats, whether the front seats in the synagogue or the back seats in limousines. Let's drop the word, and see how we get on without it.

As yourself

We were always taught that 'love thy neighbour as thyself' is the golden rule, but then I read in your website that what we call our self is usually just our ego, so it couldn't be a guide to loving our neighbour. Doesn't this mean that the golden rule isn't much of a rule? Are you setting aside the Gospel and trying to do better than it? That would surprise me and I can't figure it out, so I thought I'd just ask you.

The so-called Golden Rule is not the Gospel. Just google it and you will see how often it occurs in pre-Christian literature. It occurred, long before the time of Jesus, in the Old Testament (Leviticus 19:18), as well as in a host of other ancient texts. When Jesus was asked (in Matthew 22:39) which was the greatest commandment of the Law he quoted two passages from the Old Testament in reply, and one of them was Leviticus 19:18. He was just answering a question about the Law of Moses.

But when he spoke from himself he didn't say "Love your neighbour as yourself"; he said "Love one another as I have loved you" (Jn 13:34). There is a world of difference between the way Jesus loves you and the way someone else might love you. With all the good will in the world, when someone else loves you the chances are that their ego is involved in it to a greater or lesser extent – often to a huge extent. Our self-love is not a reliable guide to how we should love others. There are people from whom I would run a mile if they threatened to love me as they love themselves. The bottom line is that the ego doesn't know how to love. It is an excellent strategist, but it doesn't know how to love. It knows how to fish: someone puts a bit of love on a hook and casts out; then someone else takes the bait and is captured. The ego is all hooks, but real love has no hooks.

The love we see in Jesus is of a different order: it is unlimited and unconditional. The Gospel writers had to find a special word for it: *agapè*. The New Testament teaching is that by the grace of Christ working in us, we too are capable of this kind of love: love that is uncontaminated by our own confusion and neediness.

One of the greatest tragedies of Christian spirituality is that through the centuries the ego has not been seen with sufficient sustained clarity. The saints and mystics have lived beyond its grip, but we have been content to admire them rather than study how our own egos are strangling us. We cannot imitate them just by attempting to do the things they did. We can only imitate them by working (with God's grace) to free ourselves from the prison of our own egos. The world-wide interest in meditation in our own time is bringing this topic to centre stage, and this is a great blessing. The development of meditation practices may turn out in time to be the greatest blessing of our age. It is the key that is enabling Christians to unlock the treasures of Christian spirituality.

We can get glimpses of our true nature when we systematically unmask the ego and unravel its stories. The ego is the 'life' we have to lose if we are to gain life. "Those who find their life will lose it, and those who lose their life for my sake will find it" (Matthew 10:39). The life we find is the life "hidden with Christ in God" (Colossians 3:3). We could call this our 'Christ-nature' or our 'Christ-mind'.

This is a real life, not an imagined or remembered one. It is always in the present moment, whereas the ego's life is always shaped by the past. The ego is my past, my story, how I describe myself in order to remain unchanged by the present (or changed only according to my own formula). My true life is not what I look at or see in myself; it is where I look from. My true life looks through the eyes of Christ.

So, briefly, this is not about setting aside the Gospel and trying to do better, as you put it. It is a key that opens up the meaning of many obscure passages in the Gospel and allows its paradoxes to recover their fresh and practical meaning.

I'm a loser

I seem to have a knack of getting myself into problems and mistakes, haven't I? I would like to have a better relationship to God, but I don't know if I'm up to it. I know I'm a loser and I'd probably make a [mess] of that too. Anyway, take care of yourself, man.

I'm sorry that I have to shorten your letter drastically. I don't think it necessary or appropriate for everyone to know the details.

Do you like jazz? Someone said to me once that God is a jazz musician! We play a false note, and God improvises around it. God does it so skilfully, he said, that the false note is somehow just the right note.

Why do you call yourself a loser? That's other people's description of you. You told me so in your letter. You've come to believe it, and now you repeat it yourself. If you keep looking only at your own performance you will miss the game. Our life is not a game of solitaire: other people have parts to play in it. A culture of pure individualism has nothing left but competition. So it keeps telling us in a thousand ways that winning is what matters, and that losing is a disaster. What a brutal world that is: a world of nothing but competition. No friends. No God. No joy. No jazz. Just me alone. That's much worse than losing. It is missing the game completely.

You can't be a loser with God, unless you walk off the pitch. The first person in the Christian era to make it to paradise was the thief who was crucified with Jesus. Jesus enjoyed the company of sinners and failures and outcasts much more than he enjoyed the company of the religious people of his day. Those Pharisees had set up the rules in such a way that only they could win. He gave them hell (but he didn't drive them off the pitch). There's hope for everyone, even for religious people!

You mentioned your interest in making sculptures with scrap metal. I think that is pure poetry, especially in your case. I have a hunch that it is the way you are going to go. You have been calling yourself scrap, haven't you? You are that scrap metal! Your taking it in hand and making something of it is your spiritual path! This is God calling you. I want to encourage you with all my heart.

Did you know that Picasso took a turn with scrap metal? He used to go out to the city dump sometimes and collect pieces of it. He would bring them home and weld them together to make sculptures. You know how the bull seems to be a very strong symbol for Spaniards (something about macho, I suppose). Picasso found the saddle of a bicycle one day and picked it up. Then he found handlebars. He set up the saddle on the wall, nose pointing downwards, and the handlebars overhead! The bull! *El torro!* Some people might say it was still only scrap metal, but that would be like saying that music is only sound. While remaining scrap, it is also a work of art. Who but Picasso would think of it? "I don't create," he said once; "I invent." The word 'invent' means *to find*. It has nothing to do with the ego. It happens when the ego is taking one of its all-too-rare holidays. God is not only a jazz musician but a sculptor.

Enjoy every minute of it. Give it your whole heart. It is your way to God. I can feel for this better than for anything in the world. I trained as a potter many years ago. Clay is like dirt. It is so like dirt that a few well-meaning people cleaned up my workshop, once, while I was away and threw out the clay, thinking it was only rubbish. Clay is a wonderful substance. So is scrap metal. What wonderful games we play! And God is our most ardent fan!

Unique call

I have always felt that each one of us was born to do something for the Lord that no one else can do. I used to worry that I would die without accomplishing this. Now, I just pray, daily, that I will have the courage, humility, and compassion to find out what this task is and do it. Unfortunately, I can't see what it is, and this depresses me. I would appreciate your thoughts on this.

Yes, we are not parts of a machine – nor even parts of an army. An army is a group of people doing an imitation of a machine. See them marching in step: a very laborious way to walk. They want to strike terror into the enemy, I suppose, by looking inhuman. But even when we dress up in uniforms (of any kind) we are all unique children of God, and could no more replace one another than children in a family could replace one another in their mother's heart.

So yes, we are all different to our fingertips – and even our fingertips are different. That means that we don't have to try to be different from other people; we can't help being different from them (in many ways). But equally, we don't have to try to be like other people; we can't help being like them (in many ways), because we are all equally human. We are like and unlike other people. Sometimes we stress one side, and sometimes the other. But if we stress either of them to the exclusion of the other we find ourselves in very strange places.

Applying this to your call: what you are called to do for the Lord is like and unlike what other people are called to do. Let's say, for the sake of argument, that it is exactly the same kind of work: for example, caring for elderly parents. That work is uniquely yours, and no stranger could look after your parents in the way that you do. It is a unique call, even though your next-door neighbours is doing the same thing for his or her parents.

When we think of our 'calling' or vocation we usually think of a lifelong calling, a profession. But why think in lifetimes? Think in days, or just minutes. What is the Lord calling me to do today, or this very minute? It is usually not a difficult question to answer. I'm called to pick up the phone. I'm called to hold my tongue when I'd love to put someone down. I'm called to help a stranger on the street who looks lost. Such moments don't seem at all grandiose; we hardly ever think of them as a vocation – a minute-long vocation. But they are the substance of our life. We don't have to look for a unique lifelong vocation; there's enough uniqueness in each moment.

We would love to have our life all in one box, with its own label. But isn't it possible that a bit of open-hearted uncertainty and chaos might be much better? If your work is coming from the heart it is uniquely and distinctively yours; and if your heart is good, then your work will be good; it will be less likely to be a product of the ego. Of course it is possible to make mistakes, but a good heart is about the best guide we have. Someone gave me a poem the other day, called 'An Open Heart'.

> He told me one time he forgot
> himself and his heart
> opened up like a door
> with a loose latch
>
> and he tried for days to put

it all back in proper
order
but finally gave up
and left it all jumbled up there
in a pile and loved everything equally.

– 6 –

Prayer

Prayer

A few of us were discussing our efforts to pray, something we don't do too often! – discussing it, I mean. One woman said she always prayed to Jesus, but another one said she prayed just to God. Then someone asked her did she mean God the Father, or just God in general – you know what I mean. What about praying to Our Lady and the saints? Can you enlighten us?

In the gospels the disciples asked Jesus to teach them to pray. It seems a strange request. Jews prayed every day since childhood. Why would they ask him now to teach them to pray? They were asking him for a *distinctive* prayer as his disciples. John's disciples had a special kind of prayer, but Jesus's disciples apparently did not. In answer to their request he taught them the Our Father. This makes it very special: it is not just any prayer, it is a distinctively Christian prayer.

But look now: *there is no mention in it of any of the Christian mysteries.* There is no mention of Jesus, nor of his passion, death and resurrection, there is no mention of the Trinity.... What sense can we make of this? Here is how I came to some kind of clarity on it.

I remember praying a few years ago at the Wailing Wall in Jerusalem, surrounded by Jews. It Is the only remaining part of the Temple which was destroyed by the Romans in the year 70 A.D. There is a very deep nostalgia, it seemed to me, in their prayer.

> My tears have become my bread,
> By night, by day,
> As I hear it said all the day long:
> 'Where is your God?' (Psalm 41)

They have a custom of rocking back and forth as they pray. It is as if it is too much for the mind and has to overflow into the body. I thought of Jesus, a Jew, as I stood there groping in my mind for words. I realised that any Jewish person at that Wailing Wall could pray the words of the Our Father and not find them the least bit alien. Jesus was among his own people. But how then can the Our Father be the distinctive prayer of a Christian?

A long time later it came to me: if there is no mention of Jesus, his life, death or resurrection, nor of any of the Christian mysteries, it is because *this was his own prayer* – this was how he prayed himself. In prayer he was seized by a single awareness: the Father; he was not thinking about himself. When we pray the Our Father we are not praying *to* Jesus, but *with* him; we are praying his prayer. We are so close to him that we cannot see him; like him, we see only the Father. We are, as it were, inside his head, looking out through his eyes: seeing the Father, and seeing the world as he sees it. There is no distance; we don't see him somehow 'over there'. We are totally identified with him; we are indeed his disciples. We are praying *through* him. Our prayers usually end with the words, "through Our Lord Jesus Christ…."

In her *Shewings* Julian of Norwich spoke of "Adam's tunic", by which she meant human nature. It is worn by Adam, by which she means all of us ("in the sight of God all humankind is Adam and Adam is all humankind"), and of course by Jesus, since he too is a child of Adam. Jesus wears our tunic, our human nature. This phrase of Julian's is a vivid image of our 'incorporation in Christ'. We could also speak of 'the Christ-nature' or 'the Christ-mind', as Buddhists speak of the Buddha-nature and the Buddha-mind. "Let the same mind be in you that was in Christ Jesus," St Paul wrote (Philippians 2:5); and "We have the mind of Christ," (1 Corinthians 2:16). He puts it even more strongly, "It is no longer I who live, but it is Christ who lives in me" (Galatians 2:20). You could apply this to prayer and say, "It is no longer I who pray, but it is Christ who prays in me."

Have you noticed that the Eucharistic Prayers and all the prayers at

Mass (except just one) are addressed to God the Father? Then at the end of the Eucharistic Prayer it says, "*Through* him [that is, Christ], *with* him, *in* him, in the unity of the Holy Spirit, all glory and honour is yours, almighty Father, for ever and ever." The Liturgy teaches us how to pray. This is the structure, always the same. We pray *to* the Father, *through* the Son, *in* the Spirit. To pray is to be drawn into the intimate life of God – not just 'God in general', but Father, Son and Spirit.

Having said that, I have to say something else. It makes perfect sense to pray to Jesus, as millions have always done, and still do. Many people find it easier, somehow more intimate, to pray to Jesus. We can't imagine that he would somehow keep our prayer to himself. Everything given to Jesus passes through his mind and heart to the Father. The same goes for praying to Mary and the saints. It's no problem; whatever helps, helps. We're not robbing Peter to pay Paul, we are the family of God. When I was young it didn't matter who wore whose socks, so long as they fitted, more or less. That's what a family is. The blood running in the veins of the Christian family is the blood of Jesus. The Christian understanding is that we are all part of the Communion of Saints, and no one is less likely to distract you from God than a saint.

So, Deirdre, my advice is: pray any way you can. But don't forget, too, that the Liturgy shows us the great lines, the great structure, of prayer.

Ways of praying

I was at a retreat last year and the priest was telling us how to pray. It was all about … mantras. I told him that wasn't the way I prayed but he said this is the way to do it. Ever since then I feel uneasy about praying and I'm not sure I'm praying at all. I used to say an Our Father and then just sit there knowing I was close to God. Then at the end I would pray for my family and my friends and for everyone. Now I don't know what to do. I try to do a bit of what he said and a bit of what I used to do, but I end up completely restless. It has no attraction for me anymore. What's the right way of praying?

The way you used to pray sounds great to me! But that's not the point.

The point is that it was your way and it was working. You are not the first person I've met whose way of praying was disturbed by the interference of a director. I believe we should be great experimenters with ways of praying, and not bother much about other people's ways (except to see what might be helpful). The trouble with many spiritual writers and retreat-leaders, especially in the past, is that they imagined that their favourite way was the only way. But Jesus said, "In my Father's house there are many dwelling-places."

Here is what Johann Tauler (a disciple of Meister Eckhart in the fourteenth century) said about the matter.

> Do not go adopting other people's methods or spiritual exercises; that is blindness. Our various ways to God are as different from one another as we are ourselves. One person's spiritual meat is another's poison, and the graces we are given vary in many ways, to fit the needs of our particular constitutions and natures. So leave other people's practices alone. Imitate their virtues, if you like: their humility, their gentleness and so on. But when it comes to external observances, follow your own particular vocation. Concentrate on knowing what you yourself are called to do, what God is asking of you, and do that.

And here is what his teacher Meister Eckhart said. "I will tell you how I think of people. I try to forget myself and everyone and merge myself, for them, in unity." He means he merges himself in God for them. This was also the solution that St Thérèse of Lisieux devised for herself. She had been asked by so many people to pray for them that it was becoming impossible for her to remember them all. So she just said: I put all these people in my heart, and I give my heart to God; that's enough. Otherwise her prayer would become just a long litany of names.

Madame Guyon, the seventeenth-century mystic, wrote, "The Spirit of God needs none of our arrangements and methods; when it pleases Him, He turns shepherds into prophets: and, so far from excluding any from the Temple of Prayer, He throws wide the gates, that all may enter;

while Wisdom cries aloud in the highways, 'Whoever is simple let them turn in here' (Proverbs 9:4)." And her mentor, Bishop Fénelon, wrote, "Those who pray perfectly are never thinking how well they pray."

In the same vein Thomas Merton said, "Many poets are not poets for the same reason that many religious people are not saints: they never succeed in being themselves."

And a rabbi (whose name I forget; let's call him Eleazar) said, "At the Judgment God will not ask me, 'Why were you not Abraham? Why were you not Moses?' but 'Why were you not Eleazar?'"

If I quote all these people it is not to put forward a model but to reassure you that you are not alone in the way you pray, or used to pray. Go back to your own way with a good conscience, in freedom and peace.

Ransacked

I wonder if you can help me with my prayer.... I used to get a lot more out of it in the past. I used the feel very close to God and when problems arose I knew I could bring them to God.... Now I don't feel any enthusiasm about it. I put in the time, it's something I wouldn't miss, but there's no feeling in it really. Have I betrayed God in some way, do you think? Why can't I feel his presence....?

My advice is to keep going and not be surprised at anything or disappointed with anything or worried about anything. From the longer version of your letter I see that you are on a good path. A path has a lot of steps. Don't look forward, don't look back. Just keep going.

I'm not giving you this advice off the top of my head. It's the advice that the saints and mystics through the ages have given us. I'll quote a brief passage from Johann Tauler, a fourteenth-century German Dominican. He spoke of God *ransacking* your house. We might translate that as messing up your mind. The message seems to be that God isn't neat and tidy, and we can expect that our life with God will have its storms and its doldrums, and a lot of periods when nothing seems to be happening.

We must seek for the depths of our souls and we must find them.

We must go into our house, our souls…. When we go into our house and look for God there, God in turn looks for us and ransacks the house, behaving just as we do when we are searching for something, throwing aside one thing after another until we find what we are looking for. This is just what God does to us. When we have gone into our house, when we have searched in the depths of our souls, God comes and searches for us and ransacks our house…. And when I say that God seeks us in our house and ransacks it, I mean that in this house, in the depths of our souls, we are utterly deprived of all the ideas and conceptions by which we have ever thought of God before. Our house is ransacked; it is as if we had never known anything about God at all. As God seeks, for us, this happens again and again; every idea that we ever had of God, every manifestation that we have ever known, every conception and revelation of God which we ever had will be taken away from us as God searches to find us.

This is a wonderful text because it dispels all our expectations and turns the question right around: *it is God who is searching for us*. Or rather, it is a two-way search. This means that it is a real drama, and not a lonely programme of our own.

The wise ones also tell us that the God we are searching for is already closer to us than we know. God isn't like an object that is lost, sought, and then found. The process continues forever. Our whole life is a search for deeper union with God. Now I want to add something to that.

What does presence feel like? Your hands are fully present to you, never absent. But you have no particular feelings about them, probably. You weren't even thinking about them till I mentioned them. It is the same with your heart, your lungs, every part of you. You have no feelings about them. *Presence feels like nothing.* There are lots of holy people who talk excitedly about their relationship with God. Don't pay any attention the them. Above all, don't try to imitate them. Come back to the bedrock: your daily practice of prayer. Nobody else can play your part in the great drama. Tauler's teacher gave a great piece of advice: "Take everything evenly from the hand of God."

Prayer of petition

Christ said: "Whatever you ask the Father in my name he will grant you."
He also said: "Ask and you shall receive, seek and you shall find, knock and
it shall be opened for you." Why, then, do we pray for so many good things,
and rarely is our prayer answered. I believe this is the main reason why so
many of us don't pray much. Christ is not keeping his promises. What can
you say about this?

Here are a few ideas that I hope may be of some help.

In the nineteenth century a man named Francis Galton suggested
that prayer of petition should be put to the test: that one half of England
should pray for rain and then compare the rainfall with the other half.

He was not in fact the first in the world to apply the experimental
method to this subject. In the Book of Judges, Gideon said to God: "In
order to see whether you will deliver Israel by my hand, as you have said,
I am going to lay a fleece of wool on the threshing floor; if there is dew
on the fleece alone, and it is dry on all the ground, then I shall know that
you will deliver Israel by my hand, as you have said…." Gideon had the
mind of a true experimentalist: the following night he turned his experiment back to front to test God a second time: "Do not let your anger
burn against me, let me speak one more time; let me, please, make trial
with the fleece just once more; let it be dry only on the fleece, and on all
the ground let there be dew" (Judges 6:36, 39).

We know by some instinct that all this is nonsense. Prayer isn't simply
a way of getting what you want, and if you treated it as such it would
turn out to be a pretty unreliable way.

There are many people who, in reacting to the crudity of this attitude,
go to the opposite extreme of never asking God for anything – while
having no difficulty with prayer of praise, prayer of thanksgiving, and so
on. There must be a Christian attitude to prayer of petition that avoids
these mistakes.

First of all, if it makes sense to *thank* God for something, it must also make sense to *ask* God for it. But if we ask with both eyes on the goods and no eye for God, we are only acting the beggar. Prayer is not a cheap way of getting what we want; it is a way of relating with childlike frankness to the Father who knows and loves us intimately. "Why, every hair on your head has been counted" (Luke 12:7). A beggar doesn't see you at all; he has eyes only for the goods. God does not want us to be beggars, but beloved sons and daughters.

One of the most precious images of prayer that Christians have is the Gethsemane scene. Jesus went there in inner turmoil and asked the Father to let him escape impending torture and death. The astonishing calm, the dignity and trust in his Father that he showed during his trial that night and at his execution the next day, were surely the Father's answer to his prayer.

God doesn't always give us the very thing we ask for; but we trust, then, that God is giving us better. An enlightened parent doesn't give a child everything he or she asks for. A cut-throat razor, for example, might seem a great toy to a young child. Some of the things we set our hearts on may be just as dangerous and harmful to us, for all we know. But even in the case of things that are not harmful, wise parents don't always comply with a child's every wish. Their job is to rear the child, as best they can, into a loving and caring person. If they just followed the child around, satisfying his or her every wish, the child would learn to see them only as providers, not as wisdom figures. And they would be training the child to see the world as a kind of shop-window where everything could be had for the asking. The child would never learn anything about him or herself, or the parents, or the world.

God educates our desires as we ask for what we need, or think we need. But God cannot do that if we stop asking. "If you who are evil, know how to give your children what is good, how much more will your Father in heaven give good things to those who ask him!" (Matthew 7:11). Luke's gospel has a variation on this: "...how much more will the heavenly Father give *the Holy Spirit* to those who ask him!" (11:13).

What God ultimately wants to give us is the Holy Spirit, that is, God's own life. Other things are given us in relation to this.

John's gospel uses a telling phrase: asking "in my name". "I will do whatever you ask *in my name*," said Jesus, "so that the Father may be glorified in the Son. If *in my name* you ask me for anything, I will do it" (14:13, 14). "Until now you have not asked for anything *in my name*. Ask and you will receive, so that your joy may be complete" (16:24). In the Scriptures, 'name' means more than a label, it means 'presence'. There are lots of things we could not ask in the presence of Jesus. That shows that we have good breeding, and that we really are being educated by God.

Prayer of petition, again

I am a graduate student in philosophy, and it was through philosophy that I re-found and strengthened my faith. I am currently in a course on St Thomas Aquinas, and one of the things that we have been struggling with is the concept of prayers of petition. If God is immutable, and therefore cannot change his mind, and if God wills everything in one act of willing from all eternity, how, then, can prayers of petition be possible? Clearly we could pray for things to be different, but the answer has already been given (and will stay the same?), although we do not know it yet. I firmly believe that our prayers matter, but it does seem that prayers of petition can't actually make a difference.

I have just now found myself in a situation where this struggle has become more real to me than ever before, and having the answer is now more urgent and pressing. I will continue to pray, with faith, but I feel such a strong need to know how prayers of petition actually work.

It is clear that you have dived in at the deep end. Good for you: that's for brave people. I'll do the best I can; I'll try and dive in with you.

There's a short sentence that helps to keep me afloat in this deep water. I'm quoting it from memory and I'm not even sure that the words are St Thomas's, but they certainly represent his teaching. It's not easy to translate this sentence without making it cumbersome, so here it is in Latin: "*Non propter hoc Deus vult hoc, sed Deus vult hoc esse propter hoc.*"

How would we say that in English? It is not because of A that God wills B, but God wills that B should be the consequence of A. Our prayer (A) does not *cause* God to protect our family (B), but God wills that the protection of our family would be the consequence of our prayer.

Is this too clever, like slipping out of a knot? No, it's carefully balanced, and it preserves something of immense importance: it gives us a voice in what happens. Not only a voice but a hand; *we have a hand in things*. We are not puppets in God's hands; we have real power to cause things to happen. (In St Thomas's language: we are secondary causes, but secondary causality is real causality, not simply instrumental.) We are used to phrases like, "Lord, make me an instrument of your peace," but strictly speaking we are not instruments; a pen is the "instrumental cause" of the writing on a page, while the writer is the real cause. But we are not like that in God's hands. We are free agents and real causes of our actions. That is expressed in the second half of the phrase.

How can we say that God is the cause of all things – not only of their being but of their activity – and at the same time claim that *we too* are real causes of what we do? The traditional answer is that God's causality is not of the same order as ours. It is *transcendental* (because God and everything about God is transcendental).

That needs spelling out. God is not immersed in time as we are. And so God's action has no past or future. Everything God does, as Meister Eckhart put it, is done in God's "eternal Now". In other words, it's not as if God got in 'earlier' than we did and settled everything in a particular way, so that our actions can only be futile. "God *is creating* the whole world now this instant," said Eckhart. And God is acting in every action of ours. God's action no more excludes our action than God's being excludes our being. So God's causality does not exclude our real causality. Just as our being is not an insubstantial shadow, our activity (such as praying) is not like the movement of a puppet. It is really 'causal', as those mediaevals put it. But it is not competing with God's causality; it is not exercising its causality 'on' God or against God. We should say it is exercising it *within* God.

'Within God'. What does this mean? St Thomas wrote that *we are part of God's providence for the world*. (Or, in the jargon, human reason is our participation in the eternal law.) We are taken into God's counsel, so to speak, like the eldest in a family. (I've noticed that the eldest often becomes like a third parent.) Theological language can sometimes seem as cold as the instructions that come with a machine. But we know that ultimately it has to be about love – because God is love. Everything that God does *has* to be an act of love, no matter how hidden this may be from us. This is expressed much more humanly and warmly by some of the mystics, particularly by Julian of Norwich. She wrote, "In his love God clothes us, enfolds and embraces us; that tender love completely surrounds us, never to leave us." This is more accessible language than all the talk about orders of causality, but they are just different ways of saying the same thing.

I hope these few paragraphs may be of some help to you, Heather. I hope they help you to keep diving. Theological answers sometimes have the opposite effect, and more's the pity.

− 7 −
Love

As you are

A friend keeps saying to me "God loves you as you are." Almost every time we meet. She means well, but instead of consoling me it makes me feel worse. God would have to be mad to love me as I am. It's enough that the world is mad. My religion is very important to me, but I feel very discouraged with my performance as a Christian. Is there anything you can say to help me? Don't tell me God loves me as I am, because I know myself too well....

You don't mention any particular reason you feel so discouraged, so what I say will have to be very general.... Here, I'll just comment on a couple of things that struck me in your letter.

Yes, God is mad! St Catherine of Siena (fourteenth century) used to keep repeating this.

> O mad lover! And you have need of your creature? It seems so to me, for you act as if you could not live without her, in spite of the fact that you are Life itself, and everything has life from you and nothing can have life without you. Why then are you so mad? Because you have fallen in love with what you have made! You are pleased and delighted over her within yourself, as if you were drunk with desire for her salvation.

Anyone who knows anything of the Christian tradition will repeat to you, as your friend does, that God loves you as you are. There... I've said the very thing you told me not to say! *But it is a statement about God, not about you.* It doesn't say you are so good that you have earned God's love. If we felt we had to merit God's love it would be an unbearable burden, not a consolation. Our relationship with God is not an equal relationship; we are not like trading partners. If we were, there wouldn't be much in it for God, and nothing in it for us but guilt. It would be a suffocating relationship. "We can breathe again, my brothers," said St Bernard of Clairvaux to his monks, "for if we are nothing in our own hearts, perhaps there is another opinion of us hidden in the heart of God – Father of mercy, Father of those who need mercy. Why do you set your heart on us? I know: your heart is where your treasure is. How can we be nothing if we are your treasure? In your sight all are as if they were not… yes indeed, *before* you, but not *within* you – in the judgment of your truth, yes, but not in the love of your fatherly heart."

Notice that both made the same point: God loves us *within God*. It's not, then, as if we were somehow 'over there' from God, who sizes us up and decides to love us if we show signs of promise. If you loved someone as they could or should be, you would not love them at all; you would love only your idea of them. You have to love them as they are: that's where everything begins. To love them as they should be is to begin at the end. It has the reverse effect: it leaves them exactly where they are, but burdened now with guilt. When we know that God loves us as we are, we somehow become better than we are. That's the effect that love has on people.

Valerie, we're all discouraged at our performance as Christians. But can you imagine someone who wasn't! If God saw only our performance we would be in a bad way. But it is the commercial world that sees only our performance; God sees our being. It is a mercy to have come to the end of the performance: to have seen through some of our illusions, to have come to the end of our resources. It is the only way to learn something about God's grace. Thank God you have gone deeper than trading with God. Now you can enter the drama of a great love-story.

God of the penny catechism

I'm always worrying about the past, if I did the right thing…. My husband gets impatient with me at times and he tells me I have little to worry about compared to a lot of other people. But I always feel that God must think me terrible. When I think of the catechism we learned in school I wonder am I a Christian at all.... All this worrying makes my husband unhappy, and cross with me at times. He only gets cross in order to help me, he says. But I wish I could stop worrying.... He suggested writing to you. I'd be glad of any help you could give me....

I hope you don't mind that I shortened your long letter. That school catechism that you mentioned at length was republished recently. It was beaten into us as children, and some well-meaning person thought it would do us good to see it again. I looked through it in a bookshop, some 50 years after my last acquaintance with it, and I was deeply shocked. In the first chapter – which is about God – there is no mention of love! It says God is the Creator, the Lord, the rewarder of virtue and punisher of wickedness; but nowhere does it say that God loves us, much less that "God is love." What does that do to us? A God who is not love, and yet who "sees all things, even our most secret thoughts and actions," is a nightmare, and truly a horrible caricature of God. We older people grew up with that, and we pray that it didn't sink in too deeply. But it did go deep with many sensitive people.

I don't know the motives of the people who recalled this nightmare stuff to us; perhaps they believe that people are longing for old certitudes in a world of rapid change. That is undoubtedly true, and it is a good thing to get down to basics at such a time.

But the basics are the gospels, not a dated catechism. There's a sad sort of Catholic fundamentalism that thinks the penny catechism, and not the Gospel, is the bedrock of the faith. I assure you, the word that renews and strengthens us – and sets us free – is the word of God. The other thing did not come from some golden age of the past, but from a low period in Catholic spirituality. I pray that you will be healed of these wounds; and since I situate myself in the continuity of Christian preaching I apologise to you for those wounds you suffered and still suffer.

When John the Evangelist (the one who said "God is love") was a very old man he used to be brought along to speak to the Christian community, St Polycarp said. He would just repeat, "Children, let us love one another." They got tired of hearing this over and over, and they asked him to say something else for a change. "But it is the Master's whole teaching," he replied.

If we lose sight of love we lose sight of the Master, and without him there is no Christianity. The catechism looked tough and hard-edged – no nonsense – and it could make talk of love seem weak and sentimental. But Christian love is first and foremost about knowing Christ: without it, we don't know what we are talking about when we talk about God. John wrote, "The one who does not love does not know God, for God is love" (1 John 4:8). After that, it is about loving our neighbour. It is not a weak and self-indulgent feeling, but something real and practical.

Don't be surprised at this shift of emphasis from the days of the old catechism. The Christian tradition is constantly correcting itself. It is a walking along the Way (the Christian faith was known as 'the Way' before it was called Christianity). Walking, when you look closely at it, is a kind of leaning from side to side, now to this side and now to that. What you need to lean on now, it seems to me, is the love of God. "This is the love I mean," wrote St John, "not our love for God, but God's love for us" (1 John 4:10). This is the bedrock. Without it, nothing stands.

I'd suggest that you spend some time every day reading that first Letter of John. Read it as *slowly* as you can. Take one line, or even a word or two, and sit back and let them fill your mind and then your heart. Be in no hurry to get through it. Spare it: it's only eight or ten pages! They are the inspired word of God; they are God speaking directly to you. Let this wash over you and heal your wounded conscience. Most of us have consciences that are hard to get at: that may be why we were not too badly wounded! But you have a delicate conscience: you need the healing love of God all the more.

In addition to the Scriptures there is a vast Christian literature to dip into as we need it. Julian of Norwich in particular could become a special friend to you and do you much good. Ask in a religious bookshop for a copy.

Unconditional love

I hear people use the phrase "the unconditional love of God," and it sounds very wonderful to my ears. But when I read my Bible, from the very outset to the very end there appears to be always a 'condition.' In Genesis Adam is told he can eat of anything in the garden but "stay away from the tree of the knowledge of good and evil because on the day you eat of its fruit you die." And in the New Testament "No one can come to the Father except through me...." I know that the Father is not willing that any should be lost but that "all" should come to salvation; but the 'condition' seems very real to my understanding. Can you give me your view on this please?

Yes, phrases like 'unconditional love' come easily off the tongue. The language of love has a tendency towards inflation: nothing we say seems enough, so we push it and push it, forgetting that we may be undermining the value of the currency. 'Unconditional' is a bit like 'absolutely' (which seems to have replaced the word 'yes').

Still, it is about *God's* love that people use the word 'unconditional', as you say. "This is the love I mean: not our love for God, but God's love for us" (1 John 4:10). We can readily see that God's love must be unconditional, because God is unconditional – not tied to any conditions. But how, you ask, are we to understand the many expressions in the Scriptures that seem to tie it to conditions?

When we read in 1 John 5:3, for example, that "the love of God is this, that we obey his commandments," the case seems even more difficult: it appears to be more about obedience than about love.

If I had to live on a desert island and was allowed to take only one page of the Scriptures with me, I think I would take the story of the Prodigal Son (Luke 15). This was a story composed by Jesus to tell what God was like. He could have inserted any number of conditions and qualifications into the story. He could have the son pleading with the father to receive him back, and the father eventually relenting but laying down strict rules for future behaviour. It would still have been a good story. But in fact Jesus put in no qualifications or conditions at all.

The father had been scanning the horizon, missing his son, and when he saw him he forgot his years and ran towards him to embrace him. He didn't even let the son get through his prepared speech. As soon as the son began, the father said to the others, "Quick! Bring out the best robe and put it on him…."

This story supersedes everything before it in the Old Testament and is the measure for everything in the subsequent Christian tradition. But we still have to find the key to interpreting those other statements that appear less generous.

Conditions, limitations, commandments. Let's try and think about these, taking a very broad look for a start. What would our life be like if there were none at all? They have a mean look, but without them there would be no shape to anything. The idea of infinity or the unlimited didn't appeal at all to the ancient Greeks. They had a profound sense of beauty and form in everything, so the formless was repulsive to them. What would a formless building look like? Or a formless human body? What would a human action be like that had no restraint, no limits, no relation to anything around? It would be grotesque. Conditions and limitations may well serve life rather than diminish it. "True ease in writing comes from art, not chance / As those dance easiest who have learnt to dance." True ease in *living*, too, probably – true grace.

When we were young the Ten Commandments seemed the greatest restriction of our freedom, the ultimate wet blanket. In school we had to memorise what was commanded and forbidden by each of the ten, and what *else* was commanded and forbidden by each of them; that was a total of forty questions. It is interesting in adult life to see them as they really were in the Book of Exodus. "I am the Lord your God, who brought you out of the land of Egypt, *out of the house of slavery*; you shall have no other gods before me…" (20:2-3). The commandments were practical ways of *remaining free.* Any other gods would have led them straight back to Egypt.

In the New Testament the story is the same. "If the Son makes you free, you will be free indeed" (John 8:36). And then (exactly your question): "If you love me, you will keep my commandments" (John 14:15). I think it is useful to think at times of the New Testament as a 'how to' book; it is about how to remain free. St James refers to "the perfect law of freedom" (James 1:25).

Our faith is a way of living before it is a way of thinking. When someone is showing us how to do something, we are not satisfied by absolute statements about the grandeur of the enterprise; we expect also instructions that take our ability and our situation into account. So John's letter says: "The love of God is this, that we obey his commandments." This is not to say that God is interesting only in our obedience. It is not about God but about us: we are being given practical instructions.

Then your second point: "No one comes to the Father except through me" (John 14:6). Significantly, Jesus said this in response to a practical question. He had been talking about going away: "You know the way to the place where I am going." The practical Thomas said, "Lord, we do not know where you are going, so how can we know the way?" Jesus replied, "I am the Way, the Truth and the Life. No one can come to the Father except through me" (John 14:4-6). Some would like to see this statement as condemning all non-Christians to outer darkness. The correct context in which to see it is the opening chapter of John's gospel: "*All things* came into being through [the Word], and without him not one thing came into being" (John 1:3). If all things came from God through him, then it makes sense to say that all things return to God through him. This is the Christian understanding of the Word made flesh. This is a practical 'how to' for us. Non-Christians too come to the Father, but *how* they come is not for us to figure out in practice. The focus of John's gospel is always the Christian community, not humanity in general.

It is good to remember, too, that it works in both directions: it is the Father who brings us to Jesus. "No one can come to me unless drawn by the Father who sent me" (John 6:44).

What is love?

I feel I don't know what love is any more.... I always end up on my own. I've had to learn to live with my husband's remoteness.... Anyway, I never had more than a part share in him. His work was always coming up between us. Then the children... always had their own friends and were always running off to see them or going out with them... The last straw was when my daughter took off for America with hardly a thought about how it would affect me. We get breezy e-mails every week that actually make me cross. I don't expect you to know much about it but can you tell me what love means, if anything? Is it just empty talk? Does anyone care anymore? Do you have any thoughts on this subject.

I hope you don't mind that I abbreviated your letter to the text above.

I tend to agree with you that there is too much talk about love. Talk is capable of becoming a substitute for the reality. Still, it can be helpful to make a few distinctions.

I'd like to make a distinction between loving and being loved.

Everyone would love to *be loved.* There's nothing wrong with this in itself, except when it becomes the dominant theme of one's life. It feels like an enrichment, an enhancement of one's own life, a lucky stroke. But like many strong feelings – and many strong substances – it quickly becomes addictive. Then, like any addict, one has problems of supply, as well as the problem of begging and craving, and the problem of withdrawal: 'cold turkey'. I'm not suggesting that you are addicted – but addictions are a useful study: they are the extreme versions of ordinary appetites; they can show us in lurid colours what may be less visible in its ordinary shading.

Loving, on the other hand, is about giving, not about getting. If there is no twist in it, no disguised neediness, it is quite simple and straightforward. Its temperature is usually moderate, because it is our nature working as it was meant to work.

Some people so stress the difference between these – calling them 'need-love' and 'gift-love' – that they equate gift-love with pure unselfishness, suggesting that it is simply *self-sacrifice*. I would prefer to say that love is a *communion* – a communion of lives, or interests or wills or whatever. While it may often be self-sacrificing, it is not identified with self-sacrifice. It doesn't mean becoming nothing, or becoming a slave to the other. It means *becoming one with* the other: expanding oneself to include them – *as other than oneself* – in oneself.

Recently I have been reading Ibsen's play, *Little Eyolf*. The peculiar thing about it is that all the characters think of love as possessive and therefore competitive – with tragic results. Recurring motifs are *the fear of dividing oneself*, and *the need to have the other all to oneself.* This kind of consuming, predatory love is bound to end in tragedy and emptiness. The parents of Eyolf realise, after his death, that neither of them loved him. With their obsessions, that was hardly surprising. The mother saw the child only as a wall between her and her husband. The father saw him only as an ideal that he, the father, wanted to realise. "Our lives are empty wastes," says the mother at the end. A critic described the play as "a horrifying experiment in vivisection, conducted with deadly skill."

The colours of our ordinary experience are intensified by a great dramatist, but that is what theatre does. "The play's the thing…." When love is not a communion it is a fight for property. The ego's parody of love has nothing really to do with love.

I can't comment on the other things you mention, but it strikes me *from your description* that your children are normal and extravert young people, and you are lucky to have a daughter who writes to you every week despite all the excitement and distraction of foreign travel. She may be trying to cheer you up with her breezy emails. Why not *identify* yourself with her excitement and her adventures? You can do that without a visa or an air-ticket! Then her joy will be yours, and you will not feel alone in the world. It must be very difficult to be a parent. It is your way to God. May God bless you and lighten your step.

What's the motive?

I always try to help my friends and my family as much as I can by being there for them and by helping them.... But sometimes I wonder am I only doing it for myself? I mean am I only doing it to be liked by everyone...? It worries me because I must be a very superficial person if it's true.... Can you say something about that?

I notice that you used the word 'help' six times in your letter. Everyone loves a helpful person. But I understand your question: there is always the question of motives. Are you superficial, you ask. The fact that you ask the question is a sign that you are not. A superficial person has no question about superficiality.

But let's go digging! May I quote what some of the 'heavies' have said about this? Dogen Zenji (thirteenth century) wrote: "Those who do good for others, or for the future, without being noticed and without considering for whom their actions are good, are truly good persons." A rabbi said that perfect generosity was when the giver didn't know who was receiving and the receiver didn't know who was giving. It is always interesting when people who are centuries and worlds apart say the same thing. Meister Eckhart said, "When a virtuous deed seems to happen by itself, simply because one loves goodness and for no other reason, then one is perfectly virtuous and not before." There – three heavies.

Other creatures in this world don't have the difficulties that we have. They just balance their needs with their fears, and that's usually a simple equation. Then they go ahead and do what they do, without wondering how it looks or what other animals will think of them. The other animals couldn't care less, so long as it doesn't interfere with their own interests. But we are more complicated! We have the "wound of knowledge" – we are able to think and imagine beyond the facts that face us. Ordinary human consciousness is like a mirror palace: everything in us is reflected again and again, often grossly distorted. It is very hard not to look in a mirror when it is right in front of you. So we get used to checking. Soon, we can find ourselves looking for mirrors, and even feeling that nothing has reality unless it is mirrored. If we were to take it to the end we would be like film stars: all image, little or no reality. It says something interesting about our age that most of our heroes are film stars and other figures from the entertainment world.

Those people I quoted seem to say we should ignore the mirrors. That means an effort in concentration. It means giving our *full* attention to what we are doing at each moment. When I walk, let me be where my feet are at each moment, not a hundred metres ahead. When I eat, let me taste my food. When I rest, let me really rest – no TV, nothing, just rest. Then when I do something for someone, I just do it. I won't be bothered much by images and reflections. I won't even have to worry if such things are there: they will be just like insects flying around, or like sounds that don't bother me. It's easy. As Dogen Zenji said, "It is not that it is difficult to do, but to do it completely is difficult."

There, Deirdre, you get advice from two fourteenth-century characters, and from a rabbi of uncertain age. And you thought you were just writing to me!

How to fall out of love

How does one fall out of love? Lorraine

Dear Lorraine, you don't give away much information! Would I be right in guessing that the 'one' is yourself? Falling out of love: is it something you are just thinking about in a general way, or is it something you are already in the horrors of? And are you a person of few words, or is it that the subject is too painful to write longer about? Since I don't know the answers to these questions, I have to shoot in the dark. I'm sorry if a lot of what I say goes astray.

If you want to fall out of love, part of you already has: your mind and will. Then what is left is addiction. Any wounded veteran can tell you: human beings, not heroin or marijuana, are the most addictive substances in the world. So don't be shocked at yourself for getting hooked. The chances were always high that you would: there are human beings everywhere!

Are you ready for a dose of very strong medicine? Just glance at it first, and if it looks too strong, skip it. It is from the writings of a wise man, Scott Morrison.

> Our problems are not with love, but with the things we call love, which are really clinging, craving, depending, projecting, manipulating, and trying to control. These bring endless misery and loneliness. They are the process by which we torture ourselves unknowingly, out of ignorance. When we confuse and betray ourselves by pretending these have something to do with love, we trade our sweetest happiness and peace for a front row seat in any number of hell realms.

Strong medicine, but I would not make light of your pain by offering you something sweet. Why not try and learn about addiction from the experts: for example, from Alcoholics Anonymous? Their twelve-step guide to recovery embodies the deepest and most practical wisdom. Read some of their literature and adapt it to your own case. Self-pity, they know, is the trap in which many come to grief. Also: distorted thinking, resentment, rationalising…. There! – that's a practical step. They hand their lives over to "the Higher Power" every day, and they ask to stay sober just for today.

A recovering alcoholic once told me that in his drinking days he saw a large notice one evening in a pub: 'Free drink here tomorrow!' He managed to find the same pub the next day, and stepping inside he saw that the notice was still there, 'Free drink here tomorrow!' The penny didn't drop for him, and he enquired of the barman, who said, "Yes, just as the notice says: you get free drink tomorrow!" In his befuddled brain he knew that something was escaping him. The free drink was so near and yet so far. On his way to the next pub he passed a library, and on an impulse he went in and asked for an English dictionary. He wanted to look up the word 'tomorrow'. He had some difficulty finding it, but eventually he was able to read: "The day after today," it said.

Then the delayed recognition burst in on his mind. "That is stupid!" he said. "Every day that comes is *today*!" It was a moment of enlightenment. "The word 'tomorrow' (he told me) must be the only word in the English language that has no meaning!" That awareness struck him so deeply that he stopped drinking. I met him four years later and he had not touched a drop.

When you look at the future you probably see nothing but an endless succession of days without your former friend. So just look at today. Everything passes. You will be a deeper person after this. There are things that can be understood only after your heart is broken. The great Sufi poet Rumi wrote, "People often describe the process of growing closer to God as climbing a spiritual ladder. This may seem to be an apt metaphor. But only when you stumble and fall off the ladder, plunging into the depths below, do you truly come close to God."

When you begin your struggle (if you are not already in the throes of it) you may try to move, as many do, towards hatred. We have always been told that the opposite of love is hate. It is not true. To hate someone is to be deeply involved with them at the emotional level; love and hate have a lot in common. The real opposite of love is indifference. If you are attempting to hate that other person it is useful to know that the more you succeed the more you will fail; you will be even more entangled in the end. It requires something else.

The *truth* will set us free; everything else will tie us up in knots. Sometimes shout to yourself: "Cling to the truth!" – the truth of what you feel, the truth of now, the truth of your situation, the truth of the other person's situation. Don't exaggerate or put a different face on anything. Look at now, not at tomorrow. "I know a man" (to use St Paul's idiom) who on a winter evening sat alone before an image of Christ, and made absolutely no attempt to evade or explain anything; he sat in the December darkness, with nothing but the naked promise, "the truth will set you free." It was a turning point, a moment in which something very deep was learned, something to be grateful for till the end of one's life.

You know God's vulnerability now because you are vulnerable

yourself. Life is here, trembling, mortal and profoundly human. This emotional upheaval that you are feeling now is a path to God.

The Human Mix

Anxiety about the world

My niece is a single mother of a ten-year-old boy, and I lie awake sometimes thinking what's going to happen to him. The world frightens me now with all the crime and drugs and the breakup of marriages, and young people getting into drugs and sex, and all the violence you see in the news. What does the future hold for him? What chance do the youngsters have? Does anyone have any power to turn it around? I'd like to hear what you have to say about it....

When film makers don't have much of a storyline they put in lots of sex and violence. I think it's the same in real life. Many people have lost the storyline, and they go for cheap kicks to fill the void.

There's a giddy sense now that nothing is stable, that everything is moving. I experienced an earth tremor once, and it was weird to see (and feel) houses moving – the very symbols of stability. Society is like a vast house, and while we like to see a bit of change, it's very frightening when everything begins to change at once.

"Constant change is here to stay." Yes, but it doesn't stay quietly; the *rate* of change keeps on increasing, as when an object is falling from a height. We should probably say, "Constant *acceleration* is here to stay." It is technologically driven: that is what dazzles us. Every technological advance enables further technological advances; and these in turn affect our lives. There is not a lot that the ordinary individual can do to stop this or slow it down. To say this is to feel powerless, helpless....

(However, a qualification is in order here. You notice that we don't complain about advances in medicine. And we are inclined to complain if an ambulance doesn't arrive within ten minutes of being called. We all pick and choose the parts we like. Very few people are totally opposed to change and speed.)

Wherever there is speed there are bound to be accidents and tragedies. A whole society in a state of constant acceleration is almost certain to shake itself to pieces. We forget where we set out from, and we don't care where we are going. All that matters is the excitement of the journey itself. Our faith gave us the story of where we came from and where are going. Now that many reject or ignore faith, and have not replaced it with an equally compelling story, we have cut ourselves adrift.

But I don't believe we are powerless. We may not be able to change the speed or direction of change, but we can take responsibility for our own lives. You can choose to be still at any moment, even when everything around you is spinning. I read an account by a man whose life changed course as he was talking with a Zen teacher in Tokyo. There was a severe earth tremor, and people began to panic; but the Zen teacher remained completely calm. This so impressed the other man that he took up a serious practice of meditation from that day.

Without doing anything, that Zen teacher created a zone of calm that is still expanding, because that other man is now a Zen teacher in turn. We have far more influence for good than we care to believe, and if our hearts are in the right place we can create zones of calm and decency around us without doing anything. That is the purest way to do something: there is no ego involved. What you *are* will influence the life of your niece's boy; what you are is what he will remember.

"What does the future hold for him?" you ask. No one knows. The future doesn't *hold* anything; the future is nothing yet. The only thing we have influence over is the present. Pray. But don't let your prayer become just a worry session. Pray with confidence. Embody the faith of the ages. You will be embodying it for him too – because we are all one in the Body of Christ.

Your care and concern for the lad, and for our world, is already a kind of prayer. But don't let it vaporise into worry. Worry is the opposite of faith.

Anxiety about the future

I'm full of anxiety about the future – what's going to happen to my husband and me and what's going to happen to the family.... I'm always expecting sickness and accidents. I worry about money even though we have enough my husband keeps telling me.... I even worry about the dog.... I see nothing only problems in the future. I'm this way for years, and I'm very tired all the time. Is there any advice you could give me?

I hope you don't mind that I didn't reproduce all the detail in your letter. It struck me that your long descriptions were themselves an expression of fear. So I put in just the essentials (and the dog).

No one can cope with the future – because it isn't there. We can only try and cope with the present. But your *fear* of the future is in the present, and you can cope with that. That is the main thing I want to say to you.

What would your life be like now if all your fears throughout the years had been realised? You would probably have passed away many years ago. But no, you are still here. You are walking proof that dwelling on fears is a waste of effort. Because the future is never there, we can invent it and shape it any way we like – or rather, any way we fear. You have been making and editing horror movies in your head, to frighten yourself with. If you have to make movies why not make pleasant and encouraging ones? It is what most people do. So a useful question you might ask is: What is the attraction of horror movies for me? Why do I keep making them? Alfred Hitchcock made a lot of money from imagining horror, but there's nothing in it for you.

Why do we human beings like to frighten ourselves? The answer isn't obvious, so let's try and think about it. When there's a real and present danger facing us we want to see it. This makes sense: it increases our chances of avoiding it. But when there is no real and present danger – only an imagined one – there's nothing to see, of course; so we create something in our imagination that we can see. It is as if we say to ourselves, "If I imagine a lot of horrible things I may be able to avoid them." We create them in order to avoid them. It's a habit that has grown out of a real instinct, but it can grow huge and become disconnected from reality. Wouldn't it be easier for us not to create these horror scenes in the first place? They are a work of fiction. Like all fiction they are an arrangement of elements from reality without being real themselves.

All this is very general and I don't know if it is of any help. So let's try and see some practical steps you might take.

Instead of looking at your creations and allowing them to fill you with fear, look at your fear. Your creations are unreal, but your fear is real, and it exists in the present moment; it is tangible and accessible. Take up a comfortable position and relax the body. Become aware of the physical experience of fear. Don't tell yourself the stories again; keep them strictly out of it. Be aware of what fear does to your muscles. Observe it in great detail. For some unknown reason awareness relaxes tension. You don't have to do anything: just become aware. Give yourself plenty of time, and do it every day. As you become better at it you will begin to enjoy it. You will see that the body prefers not to be fed continually on fear. You will soon find that you are not exhausted all the time, because now the energy that used to go into fear (and fear is heavy on energy) is available to you for living your life.

You might look and see if there's a relaxation or a meditation group in your area. That usually makes it easier to continue; and it is always a help to know that you are not alone in your struggle. Fear is a universal human ingredient and we all have to learn how to keep it from running away with us.

I can't say, "Keep up the good work," because awareness and relaxation are the opposite of work. Enjoy the holiday!

Ageing

I'm sure there's no answer to the problem of ageing, but one's attitude to it makes a difference, I'm sure.... I'm looking back at 65, so it's becoming a very actual question for me. Could you give a few perspectives on it, please? I find your web site very helpful.

You're right, there's no answer to the problem of ageing – except what Maurice Chevalier called "the alternative". From childhood to old age we never leave it alone. When we are young we want to be old and when we are old we want to be young. Time seems like a coat that doesn't fit us properly. Not only does it not fit, but it seems to have no real shape of its own: our idea of age changes as we get older. Through the whole course of our life anyone who is about 15 years older than you seems 'old', and anyone 15 years younger seems a child.

What a mystery time is! When we want it to go fast it goes slowly and when we want it to go slowly it goes fast. I think it's the very wanting that makes it seem to do the opposite. Wanting always does that. Look at the verb 'to want': before it means 'to desire', it means 'to lack'. When I have a problem about the passage of time I have separated myself from time, as if it were something alien and apart. It appears to be over there somewhere while I am here. *But time is oneself.* (What do you give when you give an hour of your time to someone? You give an hour of yourself.) If so, then to be separated from time (wanting it to go quickly or slowly) is to be separated from oneself…. Yes, these thoughts make my head reel too!

Let's keep going, though. When yesterday was happening its name was not 'yesterday', its name was 'today'. When tomorrow comes, its name will not be 'tomorrow'; its name will be 'today'. Every day is today. There is no tomorrow and no yesterday, nothing to be gained and nothing to be lost.

I've often thought that we use the image of 'stream' misleadingly when we think of time. We imagine time as a stream that passes by as we watch from the bank. This is the spectator's view. But we are not spectators of the stream of time; we are in the stream. Picture yourself in the stream, then. You are always at the source of the stream! You are always at the very place where the freshest water is rising just now from the source. There is nothing newer than now. Tomorrow hasn't arisen, it's only a thought. And yesterday … yesterday is gone down the stream, away from you. Your childhood, in this use of the image, is the oldest part of your story! The newest part is just now. You were never younger than you are now! Don't look back to childhood for your youth; it is here and now, where you are.

I have just now by chance noticed the following passage in Kahlil Gibran's *Prophet:*

> Of time you would make a stream
> upon whose bank you would sit and watch its flowing.
> Yet the timeless in you is aware of life's timelessness,
> And knows that yesterday is but today's memory
> and tomorrow is today's dream.

Meister Eckhart wrote, "Know then that my soul is as young as when she was created, in fact much younger! And I tell you, I should be ashamed if she were not younger tomorrow than today!" If you think thoughts like this, Miriam, you'll never get a day older! – except on the outside. And the outside, as we admit little by little, doesn't matter very much.

Bereavement

My husband died in August 1998 after ten months of cancer. He was always so strong, doing everything, but in the end he couldn't lift a cup. There isn't a day but I miss him. I should be getting over it by now, but sometimes I think it happened only yesterday. I'm blessed with good friends and family who take me out and do their best for me, but it's always there when I come back. I can't really enjoy my time out with them because I know it's waiting for me when I come home. My daughter was telling me about your internet and your answers to people, and I wrote this and I'm asking her to send it to you. She has her own family and troubles, and I don't like to be bothering her. His name was Jimmy. Is there anything you could say to me that would help me?

Thank you for your heartfelt letter. It will touch the hearts of people who read it. The printed word and the internet can help create a great family that is spread all over the world, and I'm certain that very many of them will feel as if they had written the words themselves.

I showed your letter to a friend, who gave me these words for you. They are from an ancient Irish source. Your husband's name is still Jimmy; think of him saying this to you: "Grieve not nor think of me with tears. But laugh and talk of me as though I was beside you. I loved you so. It was heaven here with you." God alone knows who wrote those words, or what kind of life that person had, so long ago. But it was someone who knew the sadness of separation, and also knew that the final word about death is not separation but a new kind of presence. Life can go on, and has to go on. It need not be a constant looking back with regret; it moves forward, and there is still joy for you.

I remember the words of Peig Sayers. She had lost several of her children, yet she could be wrapped in a kind of joy. One day, walking down the hillside she was gripped by the beauty of the island and the sea, and she prayed, "Well I know your holy help, because I was often held by sorrow with no escape." She had emerged from her great sadness and could still find joy in her life.

We often say, "Tomorrow never comes," because when it comes it is today. Now, why not look in the same way at the past: at our yesterdays? We never lived through a yesterday, because every day we lived was a today! The past is not full of yesterdays, it is full of todays! I often pass the house where I came into the world many years ago. It was a nursing home then. I always think of my mother on that day, September 3, all those years ago, emerging through that door, looking much younger and holding a squalling bundle that I have to admit was me. She has been dead for 30 years, but somehow that moment (and every moment of her life) still lives, somehow, mysteriously. Everything is held in the presence of God. To God there is no past: every moment is equally present. As Jesus said, "God is a God not of the dead, but of the living; for to him all of them are alive" (Luke 20:38). He didn't say: "We can remember them and think of them *as if* they were alive;" that would only be make-believe. He said, "They *are* alive." You could say, God is their address; that's where they are to be met, that's where they are alive. Jimmy is in the care of God. We could even improve on those ancient words; we could strike out the words 'as though', and change 'I loved you' to 'I love you', and 'it was' to 'it is'.

A piece of practical advice, if I may: if you haven't done so already, change some things in the house. Don't keep it trapped in the past, because then it will keep you trapped. Put in some new things, give a few of the older things to your daughter. Every time you look at that new chair or picture, you are reminded that you and Jimmy and all of us live in an eternal Now, which is not stopped but flowing.

May it flow into ever greater and greater depth for you, Bríd, so that your pain of loss becomes an open way to God.

Happiness

[….] Why can't I be happy? I have tried so hard. I try to be friends with people, but they always reject me in the end. In the last two months alone I have been very hurt by three people, four if I counted another person who didn't look at me when I passed her on the street. I can't see what they have against me. I'm a good person and I try to do my best. I wouldn't mind if I was trying to hurt people or annoy them, then I could understand it. My mother tells me to be happy but how can I be happy with this situation? [….]

Notice that the word 'I' occurs in every sentence of your letter, including all the parts I omitted here. This is not the road to happiness. From your letter I get the impression of someone rather turned in on herself. I know that all of us are inclined to do that when we are in pain. But you won't lessen the pain by thinking more.

So what do I say? Forget about yourself? That's not a simple instruction. We can't just decide to forget. What we can do is decide to think about something else. The wisest words ever addressed to me were, "It's not about you." Life isn't about you, in this sense: it's not about the 'you' that is trying to be happy. It's not about the ego that is forever trying to establish itself and maintain itself and promote itself. There's a deeper you that doesn't care about these things. The problem is not how to make the ego happy, but how to discover your deeper identity.

You have tried very hard to be happy. It hasn't worked. Then give it up, try something else. Concentrate on something else for its own sake and not because of how it affects you. Lavish your affection on a plant or an animal, but don't stop there. Some do! Pick some old lady who has trouble doing her shopping, and do it for her for free. For free means: without looking for any kind of return. The simplest kind of return is money, and obviously don't look for that. The more complicated and demanding return is gratitude and affection. Don't look for them.

Be free, and enjoy the freedom. When you can enjoy that freedom, know that you are living from your deeper identity. You know you don't have to be grateful to yourself when you do your own shopping: you are free of the need for it. If you can be equally free of it when you do someone else's shopping, then there is no difference between someone else and you. That's how we forget about ourselves, and that's how we learn the art of happiness, and that's how we discover our deeper identity.

People have known it for a long time: "Love your neighbour as yourself." When we take care of other people, their happiness becomes our happiness, their joy is our joy. Then it matters much less how 'I' feel, or how other people regard 'me'.

Sin and forgiveness

The Gospel is simple and clear, but you clergy explain it so much that no one can understand it any more. The clergy hedges everything around with conditions and qualifications till we can no longer see the Jesus of the Gospels. You limit his mercy. "Has no one condemned you? Neither do I. Go and sin no more" (John 8:11). In Hebrews 8 we read that God not only forgives sin but forgets ("I will be merciful towards their iniquities, and I will remember their sins no more"). We read it also in Isaiah and Jeremiah. What a fine message, the mercy of God. Our sins are forgiven and forgotten, they disappear in the ocean of God's mercy. We will never be confronted with them again even on judgement day. But then you clerics get to work. Wait a minute, you say! Don't forget the "temporal punishment due to sin", even if you think you're safe from eternal punishment. And did your repentance satisfy all the conditions? And did you have a proper purpose of amendment?

No wonder many people of my generation were tortured with scruples – and some still are. No wonder people have such doubts, such uncertainty, and now such indifference. Please comment.

Yes, we Scribes and Pharisees have a lot to answer for. I remember (vaguely I'm afraid) a Herman Hesse novel in which a deceased musician's enjoyment of eternal bliss was greatly diminished by a multitude of little black and white entities that followed him around constantly. What were they? They were all the superfluous notes he had ever played. A similar fate, I'm afraid, awaits all of us who spend our lives talking.

The case you mention is the weightiest of all possible cases: downplaying the mercy of God. The revelation of God's mercy is the centrepiece of our faith, and nothing should be allowed to "hedge it around"; on the contrary everything should serve only to set it off. I remember a poem by the New Zealand poet James K. Baxter, a rare one from him about Jesus; or rather I remember the refrain.

Love – he said; and Truth – he said.
But his dearest word was Mercy.

Baxter's own life and death were a challenge to the Christians around him. He had had some kind of conversion experience that changed him from one of the glitterati to a tramp. Early one morning as he walked barefooted on a street he had a heart attack. There was nobody around, but he managed to drag himself up the steps of a religious house and ring the doorbell. Someone opened the door, looked down and saw what appeared to be a drunkard on the ground, and closed the door again. Baxter died on the steps, experiencing no human mercy in his last moments. If we ever downplay the mercy of God, it must be that we are measuring mercy by a low standard of our own. Human beings are often indifferent and merciless: the mind can dedicate itself to vengeance (calling it justice) and become a stranger to mercy. Witness the support that still exists in many quarters for capital punishment. The Church too has often been a stranger to mercy: the Papal States had their own executioner until 1870.

But the point you make is not about practice (in which everyone is a bit of a failure) but about teaching. What is the meaning of "temporal punishment due to sin"?

If you say that a lifelong cigarette-smoker is now 'punished' with lung cancer and heart disease, you are not suggesting that God is laying into him; you are saying that he is suffering the inevitable consequences of smoking. You are talking about the law of cause and effect. In various ways sin destroys our capacities: it brutalises our sensibility, pollutes the mind, weakens the will. This is not even to mention the damage it does to others. Through sin we become incapable of God and of proper human living. 'Karma' is a word that is frequently heard nowadays and little understood. But this teaching is closer to 'karma' than it is to any crude version of 'punishment'. It's a pity that the word 'punishment' is used at all. It calls God a punisher. The word 'Purgatory' comes from the Latin *purgare*, which means 'to purify', not 'to punish'.

I might add that the teaching on Purgatory is very far from the ghoulish images it normally suggests. It is in fact a powerful affirmation of God's mercy. In the following way.

Our life is for soul-making: we are to become increasingly transparent and purified, we are to become more deeply human and closer to God, we are to 'crystallise' as God's children. If I were told that this process will stop when I die, this could be very bad news for me indeed! What if I step in front of a bus and die long before I am ready? The teaching on Purgatory says that God's mercy does not run out when my clock stops: the purification can continue after death. Purification is generally a painful process, but someone in the state of Purgatory – freed now of the ego's greed and self-interest – must be experiencing ecstatic joy and gratitude. What a disaster that this should ever have been described as 'punishment'!

Sin and punishment

I heard a diatribe today from a fundamentalist Catholic about God's punish-

*ment for our sins. It sounded strange to me, for the first time in my life. I'd
like to hear what you have to say on this subject.*

Some older people have a chilling version of the 'Act of Contrition': it says
they are sorry for their sins "because they deserve thy dreadful punishments, because they have crucified my loving Saviour Jesus Christ, but
most of all because they offend thy infinite goodness, who art so deserving
of all my love…." The dreadful punishments come first in the list, so we
can't take seriously the "most of all" at the end of the lists. And there is
something sick in the occurrence of those two words 'punishment' and
'love' in the one sentence. We were being asked to love a God who would
condemn us to unimaginable torment for all eternity if we didn't love
'him'. What a way to twist people's guts! That was spiritual abuse, as
bad as any other kind of abuse. What did such a thought do to people
who really took it in when they were children?

Most didn't, I think – judging from the versions of the Act of Contri-
tion I still hear from time to time. Here is a composite of all the odd bits
I've heard: "O my God, I am hardly sorry for having offended thee, and
I do test my sins above every other evil, because they do please thee, my
God…. And I firmly dissolve … never more to defend thee, and to end
my life." In many cases a misunderstanding is a mercy.

What is at stake is our understanding of God. God is not punishment,
God is love. Commenting on St John's statement that "God is love" (1
John 4:8), Meister Eckhart said: "I beg you to mark my words. God
loves my soul so much that His life and being depend on His loving
me, whether He would or no. To stop God loving my soul would be to
deprive Him of His Godhead; for God is as truly love as He is truth; and
as truly as He is goodness, He is love. That is the bare truth, as God lives."

What then about punishment for sin? Is there no such reality? There
is! But as the *Catechism of the Catholic Church* puts it, this "must not be
conceived as a kind of vengeance inflicted by God from without, but as
following from the very nature of sin." (n. 1472) It's a pity that we use
the word 'punishment' at all. 'Consequence' would be a better word. The
consequence follows the cause as a hangover follows a drinking binge. It

is something we do to ourselves rather than something God does to us.

I found a very good image for this in the fifth-century Christian mystic, Dionysius the Areopagite. He said sin is an attempt to push God out of one's life: it is like being at sea in your little boat and seeing a great rock in your path. You reach out your oar and try to push it out of your way, but of course you only push yourself and your boat away from the rock. In his own words, "If you are standing in a boat and you try to push away a rock that is in your way, that will not affect the rock, which stands immovable, but will distance you from it; and the more you push, the more you are distanced…." God doesn't cast us away ("God is love"), but we attempt to cast ourselves away from God.

Sin and perfectionism

As I get older I find myself thinking more and more about my sinful life. I never killed anyone but I wasn't exactly what you'd call a good Christian. I dwell on it a lot. I think a lot too about all the evil in the world today…. Could you say something about this?

It is normal enough to look back, and since no one in this world has a spotless record, of course we see our sins. Our sins, like shadows, are more visible in the afternoon of our life. But we have to be careful how we focus on them: if we focus *only* on them they can bring down a gloom on the heart.

When we think of our sins *without also thinking of Christ,* the picture is all darkness. We are all too prone to wallowing in guilt instead of bringing it to Christ. This wallowing is just another way of being attached to sin. St Augustine said that if you put your sins under your feet they will lift you up to God. The Pharisees were attempting to be perfect (and because that is impossible they were attempting to *seem* perfect), but Jesus was severely critical of them, while he befriended sinners in a way that was remarkable in his time. "As he sat at dinner in the house, many tax collectors and sinners came and were sitting with him and his disciples" (Matthew 9:10). Those people, outcasts of society, knew and admitted that they were sinners, and they were therefore open-hearted, unlike the others. They came to Jesus, while the others remained at a distance, criticising.

Sometimes it is not easy to identify our sin in a practical way. There is just a vague feeling of being unworthy; it is like an unlocated pain; it is something more general than anything I could include in a list of sins. Such a feeling, left to work in us, saps our taste for God, it robs us of the energy we have for goodness. We should bring this too immediately to Christ. St Peter had to learn this, just like everyone else. His first impulse was the wrong one: "Depart from me, O Lord, for I am a sinful man" (Luke 5:8). But the Lord did not; he came, he said, not to call the virtuous, but sinners (Matthew 9:13). Read the story of the Prodigal Son: he is every one of us, including Peter. Our Father sees us when we are a long way off, "he is moved with pity, runs towards us, clasps us in his arms and kisses us tenderly, saying, 'This son of mine was dead and has come back to life; he was lost and is found'." (Luke 15)

There is another useless sort of wallowing. It is when I become pessimistic about the evils of the world: war, violence in our cities, addiction, the emptiness of popular culture…. These are terrible evils, and in your letter you detailed many of them at length – as well as all the problems in the Church. But an abstract and hopeless preoccupation with them doesn't do any good at all. If I am not actually doing something about them I am only spreading discouragement and bringing no light. It is like talking always pessimistically about the weather. Our faith is not sociology, nor journalism, nor even theology. It is *faith*, a word that means belief, confidence, trust. It is a positive and strong attitude that makes us want to move into action, not into discouragement. Our faith was known as "the Way" before it was known as "Christianity" (Acts 9:2). The way to follow the Way is to put a practical foot on a real path: help a neighbour, smile at a young person, do whatever lies within your capacity. This is easier than thinking about failure.

Crisis

I'm writing to you in desperation because I don't know where to turn.... [Everything] seems to be going against me.... I always prayed and got great comfort from it, but now I don't get anything out of it any more. I feel so alone. You would think that God would help me now in my time of need. Sometimes I think he doesn't exist at all. God loves me, my sister said, but what kind of love lets friends down? Please tell me something to give me hope. Marie

Dear Marie, thank you for your long message, and I hope you don't mind that I reproduce only a small part of it. I picked out the part at the end and I'll try to respond to it here. The particular problems, as you know, I've been discussing with you in private emails.

No, I don't think everything is going against you. You are going against everything. I'm sure you have often been advised to take it easy, not to push against everything and everyone. It was good advice. There are all sorts of things that we can't get by our own efforts, no matter how strenuous; they are *given* to us, and we have to learn to wait till they are given. "If you but knew the *gift* of God!" Jesus said to the woman at the well. If we earn something it is not a gift; and it is not a gift if we demand it, or try to force it from the grip of the person about to give it. We just have to wait – and that takes a measure of humility.

Yes, prayer can be a great comfort. But I know that sometimes it is 'comfort' in the literal sense of the word, which is 'strengthening' (from the Latin *fortis*: strong). I remember a scene in the Bayeux tapestry that showed William the Conqueror "comforting his soldiers," as the caption had it. What he was actually doing was prodding them from behind with his spear, to drive them into battle! God's 'comfort' is often like that. Think of all the things we would have run away from had we been given a choice. We are often dragged kicking and screaming into the best things in our life. I'm told I put up quite a fight the first time I was brought into a church. Many people, looking back on their lives, give God thanks that their own will was not done. We pray, "thy will be done on earth...." *God's* will, that is. But the moment it begins to diverge from our

own will, we are up in arms. When Jesus was in agony before his death
he prayed, "Not my will but yours be done." This became the headline
for all Christian prayer – in fact for all Christian life. The three who
were with him on the mountain of transfiguration – Peter, James and
John – were also with him in Gethsemane. Peter had suggested they take
up permanent residence on the mountain, but Jesus began immediately
to speak about the suffering that was to come. Every disciple can expect
to experience both Mount Tabor and Gethsemane.

We believe that God wills the very best for us. "All God's commandments come from love and from the goodness of His nature, for if they
did not come from love they would not be God's commandments," said
Meister Eckhart. Even when we cannot understand it our suffering has
meaning: it is soul-making, it is purification. It is not bad luck, and it is
not that God has forgotten about us. The world, for Christians, is not
just a place to get the most out of; it is a place of soul-making. "When
he has tried me I shall come forth like gold" (Job 23:10). This is the only
thing that can give us hope. Everything else is only a palliative.

God hasn't forgotten about you, Marie, nor let you down, nor stopped
loving you – nor ceased to exist. The same Meister Eckhart said: "What
is God's love? His nature and His being: that is His love. If God were
deprived of loving us, that would deprive Him of His being and His
Godhead, for His being depends on His loving me."

Reform

*I am appalled at the world scene, I am an old man now and when I look at
the declining standards in personal morality among the people I am angry
and disillusioned. The Church seems to be unwilling or unable to stop the
decline: those clergy who are willing are unable and those who are able are
unwilling, that is my assessment. If people cannot take responsibility for their
own lives should governments not intervene to insist on standards? In an
earlier age they would not have hesitated to do so. What is your assessment?*

I don't wish to disillusion you further, but I believe that governments are by and large more immoral than individuals. It's not difficult to think of examples, but to recite them would be to get away from the general point you make. With your question in mind I looked back over some books I read years ago, and this is what I found.

The anthropologist Colin Turnbull lived for two years with a Ugandan tribe, the Iks, and described his experiences in a book called *The Mountain People*. They are seen as utterly brutish, selfish and loveless. They never sing, and they laugh only at one another's misfortunes. They turn their children out to forage as soon as they can walk, and they abandon the old to starvation. They soil and destroy one another's property. Presumably, they were once a normal easy-going people, but the government took over their lands to create a national park, and these hunter-gatherers were reduced to farming the poor hillside soil, at which they failed miserably. Along with their way of life they lost their culture and even their humanity. It is a depressing picture.

The biologist Lewis Thomas, in *The Lives of a Cell*, sketched a theory about them – and about human beings in any society.

The solitary Ik, isolated in the ruins of an exploded culture, has built a new defence for himself. If you live in an unworkable society you can make up one of your own, and this is what the Iks have done. Each Ik has become a group, a one-man tribe of its own, a constituency…. This is precisely the way groups of one size or another, ranging from committees to nations, behave. It is, of course, this aspect of humanity that has lagged behind the rest of evolution, and this is why the Ik seems so primitive. In his absolute selfishness, his incapacity to give anything away, no matter what, he is a successful committee. When he stands at the door of his hut, shouting insults at his neighbours in a loud harangue, he is a city addressing another city. Cities have all the Ik characteristics. They defecate on doorsteps, in rivers and lakes, their own or anyone else's. They leave rubbish. They detest all neighbouring cities, give nothing away. They even build institutions for deserting elders out of sight. Nations are the most Ik-like of all…. For total greed, rapacity, heartlessness, and irresponsibility there is nothing to match a nation. Nations, by law, are solitary, self-centred, withdrawn into themselves…. They bawl insults from their doorsteps, defecate into whole oceans, snatch all the food, survive by detestation, take joy in the bad luck of others, celebrate the death of others, live for the death of others.

He concludes, "We haven't yet learned how to stay human when assembled in masses. The Ik, in his despair, is acting out this failure, and perhaps we should pay closer attention."

Note that it was a government that plunged them into this condition, by stealing their land.

There are lessons here for Christian community too. Despite hearing the Gospel, times without number, we are capable of living instead by the gospel of greed. Society breaks down around us, and we fail to create Christian community, receding into ourselves and living out our lives, Ik-like, as solitary egos. Christian spirituality challenges us to be moral, but has not been offering much towards the systematic understanding of the root of immorality: the ego. The ego cannot love, though it can produce an imitation of love, for strategic purposes. Whenever it pretends to form community with others there is a built-in flaw. As W.H. Auden once said, we have to learn to love one another or die. I don't think we can expect very much from governments – certainly not the reform of a people's morals. It is when governments claim the high moral ground that we have to be particularly suspicious of them. As Church we should look in this mirror. It is by living a Christian life of love, rather than by requiring it of others, that we stand any chance of improving the world around us.